Bringing the Steiner Waldorf Approach to your Early Years Practice

Have you ever wondered what the Steiner approach is all about, where it comes from and how it can be used to benefit the young children in your setting?

Bringing the Steiner Waldorf Approach to your Early Years Practice is an excellent introduction to this philosophy. Janni Nicol explains clearly the history of Steiner Waldorf education, the role of play in learning and the key themes of rhythm, repetition and reverence, with ideas for activities and resources. Practical examples throughout the book, involving children of different ages in a wide variety of settings, allow readers to see the connection between theory and practice.

This new edition has been fully updated to include:

- Clear comparisons between Steiner practice and the revised Early Years Foundation Stage (EYFS) requirements
- A section on the growth of international Steiner settings
- Information on celebrating festivals and outdoor environments.

This convenient guide will help early years practitioners, students and parents to really understand what the Steiner Waldorf approach can bring to their practice and to children.

Janni Nicol has worked as a Steiner kindergarten teacher in South Africa and Cambridge, UK. She is now the UK early childhood representative for Steiner Waldorf schools and kindergartens, and writes, consults and lectures on Steiner early childhood in the UK and internationally.

Bringing . . . to your Early Years Practice

Series Editor: Sandy Green

Also available:

Bringing the Forest School Approach to your Early Years Practice
Karen Constable

Bringing the High/Scope Approach to your Early Years Practice
Nicky Holt

Bringing the Reggio Approach to your Early Years Practice
Pat Brunton and Linda Thornton

Bringing the Steiner Waldorf Approach to your Early Years Practice

THIRD EDITION

Janni Nicol

Routledge
Taylor & Francis Group

LONDON AND NEW YORK

LIBRARY

Third edition published 2016
by Routledge
2 Park Square, Milton Park, Abingdon, Oxon OX14 4RN

and by Routledge
711 Third Avenue, New York, NY 10017

Routledge is an imprint of the Taylor & Francis Group, an informa business

© 2016 Janni Nicol

First edition published by Routledge 2007

Second edition published by Routledge 2010

British Library Cataloguing in Publication Data
A catalogue record for this book is available from the British Library

Library of Congress Cataloguing in Publication Data
Names: Nicol, Janni.
Title: Bringing the Steiner Waldorf approach to your early years practice / Janni Nicol.
Description: Third edition. | New York : Routledge, 2016. | Series: Bringing the . . . to your early years practice | Includes bibliographical references.
Identifiers: LCCN 2015029593 | ISBN 9781138840478 (hardback) | ISBN 9781138840492 (paperback) | ISBN 9781315732831 (e-book)
Subjects: LCSH: Early childhood education—Great Britain. | Waldorf method of education—Great Britain.
Classification: LCC LB1139.3.G7 N53 2016 | DDC 372.21—dc23
LC record available at http://lccn.loc.gov/2015029593

ISBN: 978-1-138-84047-8 (hbk)
ISBN: 978-1-138-84049-2 (pbk)
ISBN: 978-1-315-73283-1 (ebk)

Typeset in Galliard
by Swales & Willis Ltd, Exeter, Devon, UK

To my mother Estelle Bryer, Sally Jenkinson, Jill Taplin, Kevin Avison, Erika Grantham – and others too many to mention – for their sometimes inadvertent and unacknowledged contribution. I acknowledge you! Without you, this book would not be possible.

To my husband Simon and our two daughters Emma and Alexandra, with my grateful thanks for your love, patience and support.

Contents

Contents

Acknowledgements

With thanks to the many Steiner kindergartens in the UK, particularly in Cambridge, as well as to the *KINDLING* journal photograph archive for the photographs.

1 An introduction to Steiner Waldorf early childhood education

Waldorf education and early years practice today

Steiner Waldorf education was founded in 1919, and is continuing to grow and spread throughout the world, keeping true to its fundamental curriculum no matter in which culture it appears, from China to South Africa, South America to Finland. The 'early years' (known as 'Steiner Waldorf early childhood') cover pre-birth, working with parenting, baby groups and on into kindergarten (3 to 6 plus years). Steiner Waldorf schools offer a real alternative to mainstream education throughout the world, and see themselves not as competitors but as partners, providing a complementary provision, contributing to and learning from other educational practices. In many countries, such as Norway, Sweden, Denmark, Germany, Holland, New Zealand and Australia, Steiner Waldorf schools are publicly funded within the maintained sector. Steiner kindergartens thrive in Europe, (particularly in Germany where they were established originally), where they are an accepted part of education. New initiatives for training Steiner Waldorf early childhood teachers are springing up all over the world, particularly in the Far East, where new kindergartens are growing and spreading.

In the United Kingdom, there are now publicly funded Steiner schools, and in 2009, the Steiner Academy, Hereford, became the first fully funded Steiner school as an Alternative Provision Free School (i.e. Academy). There are now four academies (and more in the pipeline), all of which have kindergarten provision. Steiner kindergartens receive Nursery Education Grant funding through their Local Authority, and all work within the Early Years Foundation Stage (EYFS), as this is a statutory requirement. Teacher training is offered for all stages of the curriculum. Steiner kindergartens can be registered as independent, or attached to an independently registered Steiner Waldorf school, as part of their early years department.

Birth-to-three work is growing, and there are also new day-care centres being established, as well as growing work with the 'Pikler Approach', which is being integrated into the birth-to-three work (further information in Chapter 11). There are a number of Steiner-inspired childminders who have also completed the Steiner (EYE) training.

Steiner Waldorf education aims to respect the essential nature of childhood and, in the early years, a secure and unhurried environment enables children to develop a range of skills, which provide a sound foundation for emotional, social and cognitive intelligence later. A highly trained Steiner practitioner (usually referred to as a 'kindergarten teacher') encourages the child's creative play and self-motivated enquiry, and offers themselves as an example rather than an instructor. Through imitation, children naturally develop a sense of their own purposeful doing and creating alongside the working adult.

In the pre-school years the inner activities of thinking, feeling and willing (doing) are largely undifferentiated. The young child thinks in doing and expresses their feelings spontaneously in word, gesture and action. At this age children learn by doing and especially in joining in what is being done by others. Within the kindergarten, learning experiences are embedded within the business of daily living, and a great range of domestic and creative (artistic) activities are offered in an informal way, allowing enthusiasm and initiative to flourish. The kindergarten environment provides a quality sensory experience, and is equipped with simple natural materials and toys, enabling the child to develop their spontaneous play, which arises from within the innate creativity of each child. Within the rhythmical structure of the day and week, regular activities are repeated. A sense of familiarity enables the child to learn new skills without undue stress, allowing them to feel secure and confident. Opportunities for reverence, to experience awe and wonder, are developed through respect for each other and the environment. The oral tradition of storytelling, puppetry, music and movement, rhymes and songs, develop memory and a rich imagination.

In the first seven years, the education works with the developing child's innate rhythms in such a way that they develop a strong physical body, good motor skills, as well as a healthy regard and respect for each other and the world in which they live. These first seven years are a time for children to experience an unpressured childhood, in a place where they can grow in peace and harmony, feeling safe and not under pressure to perform or compete. Within this protective and homely mixed-age environment a rich tapestry of essential lifelong learning experiences can be slowly woven, before formal teaching is introduced at around 7 years old. In Steiner Waldorf education, we call this place the 'kindergarten' or 'early childhood environment'.

2 | A brief history of Steiner Waldorf education

Rudolf Steiner was born in Kraljevec, then part of Hungary, now Croatia, in 1861. He was intensely awake to nature, and was convinced of the reality of an inner life. He studied science and the classics, and tutored pupils in the humanities. Philosophy, science, literature and the arts were his principle interests, and he gained his doctorate in Philosophy.

The extraordinary originality of Rudolf Steiner's mind led him to a philosophy which linked up the world of science with that of spirituality.

Figure 2.1 Rudolf Steiner

His revolutionary ideas (called 'Anthroposophy') took form in a number of enterprises, among which are art and architecture; biodynamic agriculture (organic farming working with natural rhythms); anthroposophical medicine (an extension of orthodox medical practice, including Weleda medicines and toiletries); curative education and social therapy (including the Camphill movement); speech and drama; Eurythmy (an art of movement making speech and music visible); virbela flowforms (water purification systems); ethical banking; and education.

The Waldorf method of education

The first Waldorf School grew out of the political and social devastation throughout Europe following the First World War. In 1919, Emil Molt, an industrialist and the founder and managing director of the Waldorf Astoria Cigarette factory, in Stuttgart, Germany, asked Rudolf Steiner to provide an education which could offer a healing to mankind:

> It is essential that we develop an art of education which will lead us out of the social chaos into which we have fallen. The only way out of this is to bring spirituality into the soul of human beings through education.
>
> (Steiner 1968:11)

After a period of intensive teacher training, the first truly comprehensive, non-selective, non-denominational school, 'which could provide for the children of workmen and employees the same teaching and education as that enjoyed by children of families with means' (Molt 1975: 137), was founded, starting the growth of Steiner education throughout the world. This educational impulse roused particular interest in England, where Steiner was invited to lecture. Here, he met many educationalists, forming a warm and mutually respectful friendship with Margaret McMillan, the founder of the 'nursery schools', and who achieved so much in the field of early childhood education and care in Britain in the early 1900s.

Rudolf Steiner passed on his ideas for the kindergarten to Elisabeth Grunelius (1885–1989), a Froebel-trained kindergarten teacher (see Chapter 3), who took on a kindergarten group in Germany for a temporary period in 1920, and then established the first Steiner kindergarten in 1926, in Stuttgart. She worked closely with Steiner in establishing the fundamental principles for Waldorf early childhood education before his death in 1925. The school was closed by the Nazis in 1938, and in 1940, Elisabeth went to America, where she founded Steiner Waldorf kindergartens. In 1947, she returned to Germany to work with Klara Hattermann and others, who were expanding the work in Europe. She gave support to teacher training and started the first international kindergarten conference in Hanover in 1951 (which continues today). Her book, *Early Childhood Education and the Waldorf School Plan*, was published in America in 1952.

Steiner Waldorf early years

The kindergarten

The word 'Kindergarten' originated in the nineteenth century with the German educationalist Friedrich Froebel (1782–1852). The literal translation from the German *Kinder-Garten* means 'Child Garden'. 'Garden' in German is connected with the word that means 'to bend' (transform, metamorphose). Froebel used this concept as an inspiration for the child's environment; namely a 'Paradise Garden'. It is a common term for early years settings in many countries throughout the world.

Children attend the 'kindergarten' between the ages of three and six. In many schools or attached to kindergartens, parent and child groups and pre-kindergarten groups (often called 'pre-kindy' or playgroups) are provided for younger children (2 to 3 or 4 years old). There are a number of nurseries or full day care which also cater for babies upwards, and run all day. Group sizes vary and are compliant with statutory regulation. Traditionally, in the kindergarten years, five morning sessions per week are offered, each session lasting for approximately four to four and a half hours. Children take up provision according to age and need, but by five they are expected to attend five 'days' a week. Wrap-around or afternoon care is often available if required, and in some day-care centres they form a continuous provision until 6 p.m. Increasingly, providers are exploring the need for wider early childhood provision with Steiner Waldorf nurseries and all-day kindergartens, and the move to the Children-Centre concept – combining health, care and education and working specifically with parents – is an idea particularly compatible with Steiner education.

General educational principles

The seven-year periods

Steiner divided the broad principles of child development, and the educational methodology supporting it, into three psychological and physiological phases of childhood, each approximately seven years in length. These indicate a change, both physically and mentally, at around the age of 6 to 7 years; the second period, including puberty, to 14 years; and the development to adulthood culminating at around 21 years old. Although each stage has a precise integrity, processes coming to a certain culmination in one phase transform into faculties in the subsequent stage of development. An example of this is that the forces so strongly at work in building up the physical body (often referred to in Steiner education as 'the hand') in the first seven years, become available as the basis for healthy cognitive development later on (the 'head'). This threefold approach involves holistic support for the development of the all-round human qualities of willing (doing), feeling (emotions) and thinking (cognitive); in truth, an education of hand, heart and the head.

The first seven years

Social, emotional, cognitive, linguistic and physical skills are accorded equal value in Steiner Waldorf early childhood education, and many different competencies are developed. Activities reflect the concerns, interests and developmental stages of the child, and the carefully structured environment is designed to foster both personal and social learning. The curriculum is adapted to the child and takes as its starting point the careful observation of the nature of the growing and evolving human being seen in their physiological, psychological and spiritual aspects, and focusses on the inner nature of the child, rather than theoretical or ideological aspects.

This view that physical, emotional and cognitive/intellectual development are subtly and inextricably linked underpins and informs the early childhood curriculum, which is tailored to meet the child's changing needs during each phase.

Developmental stages

At each developmental stage, the child presents a particular set of physical, emotional and intellectual characteristics which require a particular (empathetic) educational response in return. This is the basis of child-centred education. The formative period before second dentition (5 to 6 years) is seen as the period of greatest physical growth and development. Structures in the brain are being refined and elaborated – a process which is not completed until around 6 to 7 years – and until that time the young child's primary mode of learning is through doing and experiencing; the child 'thinks' with the entire physical being.

Early learning

This early learning is mostly self–motivated, allowing the child to come to know the world in the way most appropriate to their age: through active interaction, feeling, touching, exploring and imitating; in other words, through 'doing'. Only when new capabilities appear, at around the seventh year, is the child seen to be physically, emotionally and intellectually ready for formal instruction. Through experiential, self-motivated physical activity the small child 'grasps' the world with their entire being in order to understand it: an essential pre-requisite for the later activity of grasping the world through concepts. Children are encouraged to master physical skills (sewing, sawing, building, baking), before abstract intellectual ones (reading and writing).

The formative forces

The core idea relevant for the first seven years is that the formative forces – those working on the development of the physical body, the brain and nervous system, in the sense organs, in walking and motor coordination, in linguistic development and the establishment of behaviour patterns – are freed up in and around the seventh year, and become available for other developmental processes. At the end of this phase of development, these formative processes become active in the different capacities for thinking, feeling and willing. This is particularly apparent in the development of cognitive and intellectual faculties. Increasingly, the child is able to direct and focus attention for longer periods of time, which is essential for the challenges of formal learning. This is accompanied by the increasing ability to form active mental images at will, which is vital for the mastering of abstraction which is needed for cognitive activities associated with reading, writing and mathematics.

It is a primary principle of Steiner Waldorf education that formal education is only introduced at the point of the transformation of these formative forces. The premature engagement of these forces in early intellectual learning can lead to the weakening of the physical forces of regeneration, and possibly also to a tendency to certain learning difficulties. Today, young children are exposed to many influences that weaken their constitution and call prematurely upon their formative forces and vitality. The extra stress of early academic learning can seriously undermine their overall development and well-being. Steiner Waldorf education sees the establishment of the seven-year rhythm, from birth to

Figure 3.1 Imitation and example

twenty-one, as an important cultural pedagogical task that can help children strengthen their inner forces and harmonise their development.

Imitation and example as an educational approach

The kindergarten is a community of 'doers' supported through meaningful work: for example, baking bread or working in the garden. The children are welcome, but not required to help. The activity of the teacher may inspire the children to become independently active, finding their own learning situations in play. Children perceive and register everything the adults do: it is not only *what* is done before the young child, but also *how* it is done. Teachers are conscious of their own moral influence upon the child and of the development of good habits through imitation:

> . . . before the second dentition (the child lived mainly) in the region of the will, which was intimately connected with the child's imitating its surroundings. But what at that time entered the child's being quite physically, also contained moral and spiritual forces that became firmly established in the child's organism.
>
> (Steiner 1988:116)

This means that the will of the child can be developed and become strong through good habits, consequences and limits set by the adult as their example.

Working with the will

The ability to implement intentions, to do what you have put your mind to doing, requires discipline, resolve and a sense of purpose: an action with purpose, focus and intention! This is what we call 'working with the will', and this, in the early years, takes two forms: the child's will is *activated* by the image of the adult engaged in activity; and the will of the child is *engaged* by the purposeful work of the adult. When the adult is involved in their own work (usually domestic) this creates an environment which is already active. The child is totally free to either join the activity or task with the adult, and work out of imitation following the adult's example, or, by being in this already creative and active environment, to become involved in their own child-initiated free play. Here the adult can establish an orderliness, rhythm and good habits. Imitation is will activity; it cannot be taught, but has to be done 'out of' one's own will.

> There was a five-year-old girl in my kindergarten who, each time she did a drawing, perhaps only one a day, rolled it into a scroll and tied it with a piece of wool to take home to her mother. After a few weeks of wrapping, rolling and tying all sorts of knots, she asked to be shown how to tie a bow. For the next few days, all she did was tie up pieces of paper – 'making presents for all her friends', she said – but it was the tying of the bows which was the driving force. She did not join in any play, but just sat at the table tying and tying these parcels. Once she had mastered the bow-tying, she lost interest and went on to play with friends, as if this never happened.

Will activity is very individual, and we can observe this in the different ways children imitate. Even if each child sees the same example of a working adult in front of them, their reactions might be quite different. Some children may immediately start to imitate the adult at work, or to play near the adult, taking in the atmosphere of the working activity, while other children don't get the impulse at all, and will sit comfortably working alongside the adult, watching the play. Within imitation there is freedom.

The child is engaged in a natural way when we are, as adults, involved in meaningful activities worthy of imitation: tasks which have a purpose and an end product that enhance the well-being of others and ourselves. Where possible these tasks should also be completed and not left half-done.

Taking part in any activity helps with learning, and we use technology which is integral to the activity, such as real woodwork equipment, grinders for making flour for bread, blenders for making soup, scales for weighing, weaving looms and cookers for baking.

The activities are divided into two areas: domestic and artistic.

Domestic activities

These enhance the physical body, and are often referred to as 'life arts'. They involve archetypal movements and activity, much of which is lost in today's home environment. Making bread, the physical act of kneading the dough, brings it alive: the ingredients, the feel and the outcome: taste, smell, texture and sheer enjoyment! Here, bread-baking becomes an activity which is both educational and worthy of imitation, and also engages the will. The children work through the process of first planting the grains of wheat, watching and cultivating the growing wheat, harvesting, winnowing, threshing, grinding it, and adding the ground flour to the flour with which they bake. They weigh, measure, count, stir, watch the yeast rise and mix the dough. They knead it, bake it and finally eat it. A 'whole' process.

This process is repeated weekly, on the same day, and the weekly rhythm and repetition also works to harmonise the active will forces.

Another example of engaging the will in domestic activity is sweeping or dusting. This also raises questions: Where does the dust come from? Where does it go? There is a beginning and an end, which is satisfying to the child, *and* a harmony in the archetypal movements. Scrubbing and cleaning the table before eating, washing, mending, cooking, decorating, gardening, tidying – these are all domestic tasks worthy of imitation because they have a positive outcome and are on a level the children can understand. These are good for the well-being of the physical body: the children re-enact reality until the skill is acquired, becoming good citizens in the process.

These activities are also important in the home, where the child has the opportunity to clean and tidy (even if it does take forever). It is the process that is important, not necessarily the outcome: these are life skills which enable us to contribute not only to our own self-development, but also to society and the earth.

13

Figure 3.2 Preparing the snack

Artistic activities

Artistic impulses arise within us if we are provided with the right environment. They can be healing to the soul, therapeutic, uplifting and enlivening. Artistic activities are provided in the kindergarten, enhancing creativity and enriching the inner life: for example, stories told by the teacher (not read) which give space for the creation of mental pictures, using imaginative faculties. Other activities that are provided and which feed this inner life are: singing, poetry, music, storytelling, puppet shows, painting, drawing, modelling, etc. While doing these artistic activities, the child is able to respond freely out of their own creativity. Anyone watching children involved in an artistic activity are amazed at the capacity for involvement and creativity which comes out of their own inner, imaginative activity.

- **Crafts** such as weaving, woodwork, sewing and others, which the children complete for gifts and celebrations, are often seasonal, and are generally made with materials found in nature. Sheep's wool – washed, dyed and carded – can be spun, woven and felted. Tissue paper is used to make birds, butterflies, flowers and other decorations. Lanterns are made for the Martinmas festival, and at Christmas, the children make presents and decorations for their families and home that are sewn or sometimes made out of wood or other materials.

Painting is done in a particular way; it is generally called 'wet on wet' painting. Good-quality paper is soaked in water and sponge-dried onto a large board. Diluted watercolour paints are used in the three primary colours, and these are placed on the table with a jar of water and a sponge for wiping the brush. The children sing a painting song before beginning, and the mood is always peaceful and dreamy. The paint brushes are an inch wide and quite long, and the children 'stroke them like a pussycat', imitating the teacher as they paint with them. As the paper and the paints are wet, the colours run into each other, and the children are delighted to discover that they have 'made' the secondary colours as they mix

Figure 3.3 Painting activity

together: red and blue make purple; red and yellow make orange; yellow and blue make green; and altogether they make . . . mud! The children wash their brushes in the water and dry them on the sponge before putting them into the next colour, and when finished, they carry their paintings boards to the rack to dry. With painting, in particular, it is the process which is important, not the outcome.

- **Drawing material** is generally accessible. However, drawing as a joint activity sometimes takes place. The teacher draws with the children, using good-quality white paper on a drawing pad. Block and/or stick crayons are made from beeswax and plant colours, and black is seldom used. (These crayons are particular Steiner equipment: see Suppliers, Appendix 2). The children sometimes imitate the teacher or each other, and at other times, they draw part of a story told before the activity, or a picture out of their own creative impulse. Using the crayons promotes the use of good pencil-holding skills, and the flat blocks mix the colours together and cover the paper easily. The corners of the paper are often rounded, providing a harmonious frame for the picture.

Implicit learning

During the early years, teaching is by example rather than by instruction or direction, relying on the child's innate power to imitate (a mirroring which the child takes deeply into themselves). Understanding the imitative nature of the young child is the key to teaching and discipline. Learning is 'caught rather than taught'; in other words, the emphasis is on implicit, informal rather than explicit, formal teaching. Children learn through participation and imitation in the meaningful context of the rhythms of the seasons, and the daily activities within the framework of the week. This approach distinguishes itself from formal learning in which children are made aware of what they have to learn. Progressions are planned and live in the consciousness of the teacher but are not made explicit. Only older children in their last year of kindergarten are expected to accomplish some tasks which are given. Within this time, however, there are many transitions from informal to more formal learning.

Providing the child with a positive model to imitate, means that all the adult's actions, deeds and even thoughts, should be worthy of imitation by the young child.

The child's whole body is a sensory organ uniting external impressions with their internal world; similar to the function of the eyes. Eyes themselves do not see but act as mediators through which we see. Everything the child absorbs, therefore, reflects on their development: physical, social, psychological and organic. Every perception is first deeply assimilated, then grasped with the will and reflected back in echo-like activity.

This interaction of external impressions with the child's internal organic development is revealed in the wonderful power of imitation, with which every healthy child is born.

Important priorities therefore arise for parents and educators (parents are the child's first educators) in selecting and/or filtering the impressions which confront the child, providing only impressions which are worthy of imitation:

To provide this protection we need to be aware of the effects of impressions:

- Physical: such as suitable clothing (natural fabrics), touch (gentle), materials and toys (organic forms and natural materials).
- Emotional and behavioural: such as avoiding arguing, shouting, emotional tension; physical behaviour which is gentle (no hitting).
- Sensory: we need, as far as possible, to filter the impressions which confront the child, such as those from television, radio, music, traffic.

We ask, is what they are confronted with in daily life what we want them to imitate, to absorb and to become?

From a pedagogical point of view, if we are aware of the child's innate power of imitation, it requires that we become good role models, encouraging the right impulses through our actions. We can become aware of our behaviour: how we apply ourselves to our work in home or garden; in the way we take care of and speak to each other; and in the way we develop and care for our environment. Anyone interacting with the child becomes part of the educational process of that child.

Phases of imitation in development

In the first six to seven years the imitative behaviour of the child passes through three distinct phases, connected with the forces of organic development which influence the whole body:

First stage: 1 to 2.5 years

During this time the children acquire three of the most important human abilities: to stand upright and walk; to speak; and to think in words.

They do this through imitation (children deprived of human contact do not acquire these human abilities in a normal way). The child during this period uses their will forces unconsciously; everything is done without reflection or consideration, it is done simply out of imitation and habit. What children observe determines how these habits develop. At the same time, they will experience how far they can go. If the adult picks the rattle off the floor when the child throws it from the high chair, the child will automatically do it again and again, seeking the adult's attention, as well as developing the skill.

It is so important to provide simple toys at this stage, such as natural organic forms – for instance, wooden logs, shells, conkers – which will stimulate them imaginatively (see Chapter 4). Toys with mathematical fixed forms, or which are complete in themselves, do not stimulate the child's formative and imaginative forces.

Second stage: 3 to 5 years

Around this age, two new faculties develop: imagination and memory. Children begin to use things around them in a different way, transforming and creating with the objects in a new way each time. What was previously a round slice off a log now becomes a wheel or a plate. What they observe from their surroundings is now imitated in their play.

> As the muscles of the hand grow firm and strong in performing the work for which they are fitted, so the brain and other organs are guided into the right lines of development if they receive the right impressions from the environment.
>
> (Steiner 2008:32)

Third stage: 5 to 7 years

The forces of development most strongly at work during this time are those which drive the child into self-initiated activity – the 'will forces' – which become more conscious. At around the age of five, the child experiences what could be called an 'inner boredom'. It is as if they have been abandoned by their imagination, and often the cry of 'I don't know what to do!' is heard. Children begin to lose that innate imitative power, and their thinking emerges in a more conscious way. It now becomes important to encourage them to participate more in adult activities: cleaning, washing, sweeping, cooking, sewing, woodwork. Then transformation takes place and the children begin to play out of an inner picture, as a preconceived image. They plan their play and it becomes more organised.

It is therefore really important to create spaces which allow children to play creatively and provide opportunities for imitation. The outside world is observed and reflected in the play of the child who then re-enacts this observation over and over until a particular skill is acquired. This can also work in a negative way if they are exposed to negative images, behaviour or violence in their surroundings or in the media, to swearing or other aggressive behaviour. In the kindergarten it is all too often played out in some form. Sometimes the child has to re-enact it in order to understand it or experience it themselves, or sometimes simply to work it out of their systems. For instance, one can often see the whole kindergarten moved around during the free play time when a child has just moved house!

A picture of the development of the will forces is clear in the following description, from Joan Almon, a kindergarten teacher from the USA.

A six-year-old boy who built himself a car in the kindergarten was now trying to find a way to steer it. The car was made of two stumps of wood which had been turned on their side with a wide board lying across them. If he straddled the board and pushed with his feet he could make the car roll a bit, but he could not steer it this way. On this particular day he wanted to find a way to steer it and spent 45 minutes trying to tie a rope onto the stumps and onto the board in such a way as to connect the two and manoeuvre it. Again and again he tried it, first one way and then another. At last he gave up, and with a shrug dropped his rope and went off to play with a friend. One felt he had learned as much from a seeming failure as he would have from a success. One day he would realise that an axle and a drive shaft are needed for this step, which a simple rope could not accomplish. In the meantime, he had fully directed his will to the task and seemed not at all frustrated by his inability to make it work.

In the kindergarten, opportunities are provided for the child to play out their observations by allowing the space and time for child-initiated play with simple materials, which can be adapted using their fantasy and imagination. It is best achieved by the presence of purposefully occupied adults, where children can be 'securely enveloped' by adults' work. The adult thus occupied provides a rhythmical and ordered structure, demonstrating enjoyment of work as well as the willingness to work hard. However, as you can see in Chapter 4, the teacher has plenty of opportunity to guide this play should it be required.

Figure 3.4 Building a car

4 | Play

The serious work of childhood

Play embraces children's total experience. They use it to tell their stories; to be funny and silly; to challenge the world; to imitate it; to engage with it; to discover and understand it; and to be social. They also use play to explore their inmost feelings. In a single game – playing alone or with friends – the child can switch play modes, one minute imitating the television, the next making a discovery which leads to new thinking, then being reminded of something else and changing the play accordingly, and suddenly being swamped by feelings, which require their own corresponding set of images, propelling the game in yet another direction. Like dreams, play is not ordered and rational. It does not give priority to one kind of experience or one kind of knowledge over another.

(Jenkinson 2001:42)

The *Start Right* Document on Nursery Education (Ball 1994) laid down that 'play is the serious work of childhood'. In a time when play was (and sometimes still is) regarded as any pre-prepared activity used as a learning tool to predetermine an outcome (the 'learn as you play' model), Steiner education took the view that this deprives the child of the freshness and nourishment of freely chosen, open-ended play; that really creative play is unpredictable and has endless outcomes. Today, this child-initiated play is accepted as necessary for understanding observed activity and integrated concepts.

Children still live in a dreamy world full of feeling, and their own feelings are still largely unconscious, which is why they can imitate.

Through this imitation of the world around them they can learn from life. The play is thus continually moving and creative, and with endless educational content. The following is an example of this open-ended play from my kindergarten in Cambridge:

Ike had built a van. He was a builder. There were two seats in the van and the children were keen to join him. Owen got his tools and shared the driving. They had piled up chairs to sit on (vans are higher than cars) and the front of the van was a bent screen across which they had balanced a plank. The steering wheel (a slice of round log) was placed on it, and there was a brake, accelerator, etc. made of wooden blocks. Ami wanted a ride to the safari park, and Owen kindly made space for her. They 'drove' this van to the park, and then needed binoculars to see the animals. Ike and Ami fetched paper and string, and made binoculars which they took back to the van, which Owen had been looking after. By this time, other children, interested in the play, had joined them. Owen directed them into becoming animals in the park, and they had to build pens to keep them separate. Another child decided to feed the animals, and put conkers into bowls, pushing the bowls carefully under the screens which 'penned' the animals.

This play lasted for around an hour, continuously growing and changing as children joined in, and during this time the adults sat at the table preparing the snack and observing. There was no need to interfere, guide or lead this play in any direction, as the teachers' work was to observe the children in their play, not to continuously interrupt to ask questions or 'tick' responses; the creative process was interfered with as little as possible.

> Children who show the greatest capacities for social make-believe play also display more imagination and have less aggression. They also have a greater ability to use language for speaking and understanding others, show more empathy and are able to see things from the perspective of the other; and show less signs of fear, sadness and fatigue.
>
> (Klugman and Smilansky 1990:35)

23

There are many different forms of play, including:

- socio-dramatic play
- solitary play
- exploratory play
- play involving leaders and followers
- play which follows a 'script' (e.g. a TV show)
- re-enactment of stories
- animal play
- floor play
- outside play
- scary play
- daring or risky play.

So what do children gain from creative play? Below are a few suggestions:

- They learn to negotiate;
- They learn to change ideas;
- They learn about relationships and emotional responses;
- They learn to deal with success and failure;
- They learn to improvise;
- They learn to create anew;
- They learn to understand and think;
- They learn concentration;
- It supports physical, emotional and social development;
- It strengthens imagination;
- They learn through investigation, exploration and discovery;
- It encourages inventiveness and adaptability;
- Problem-solving;
- Practical skills;
- They learn to use self-control;

- They learn to share and take on the perspective of others;
- It develops language and communication skills.

In *The Importance of Play*, a report on the value of children's play, Dr David Whitebread writes:

> The evolutionary and psychological evidence points to the crucial contribution of play in humans to our success as a highly adaptable species. Playfulness is strongly related to cognitive development and emotional well-being. The mechanisms underlying these relationships appear to involve play's role in the development of linguistic and other representational abilities, and its support for the development of metacognitive and self-regulatory abilities.
>
> (Whitebread *et al.* 2012:5)

Play requires imagination and fantasy, the very foundations of flexibility and creativity which also promote self-confidence and self-esteem.

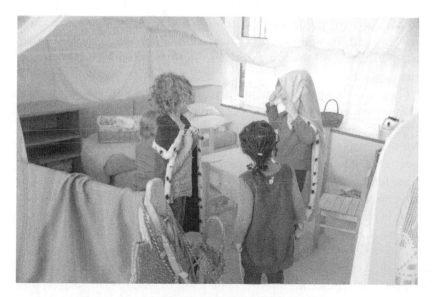

Figure 4.1 Social play

During the kindergarten morning time for free play is therefore given priority (both inside and out).

Play and child development

The child under three plays realistically: they imitate the world around them. They have to find out what the earth is made of, how it works, who the people in it are, how do they work. They need the involvement of adults to imitate, or to play with, and are involved with the activities of the mother, father or others around them. They play repetitively, building the brick tower and knocking it down again and again, with joy each time, before moving on to the next thing, and interact enthusiastically with their surroundings, finding each experience fresh and exciting. Very young children tend to play alongside each other, involved intensely in their own individual experiences, and only interacting socially when another child enters their space. I remember my daughter's favourite activity at this age was emptying and sorting the container cupboard, while I was busy in the kitchen: piling up the empty storage tubs, finding the lids which fitted, banging them with a wooden spoon and only putting them back when I made a game with her of stacking them back into the cupboard.

Between the ages of three and five the children's ideas and imagination are triggered first by the object or toy, and then by some memory, which brings the object into play. A footstool could be a table set for a tea party to which a friend would be invited, and shortly after, could become a doll's bed when upturned and filled with a cushion: time for a nap after tea! In order to play in this way, children need to have experienced these things already, and so recreate them in play. Play is now stimulated by external events, and this is why it is important that there are toys or objects available to the children that can be transformed by them into anything they wish them to be. That cut-off slice of round log could become a tray, a plate, a steering wheel, a computer keyboard . . . or a log to build with! (See section below on toys). Now play is more social, children interact and need each other to transform and mould the play. They are stimulated by each other's ideas and experiences. They begin to negotiate, learn boundaries and limitations, investigate possibilities, build their language and communication skills and hopefully learn to empathise and care for each other. They play with increased concentration, but the play can still result in chaos, and often needs intervention or direction from the adult: a guiding hand to extend the play or help with social interaction.

Being involved with the domestic activities in the kindergarten also stimulates play at this age, and joining the adult in the washing of the dolls clothes, for instance, often leads to extended play: for example, in creating the right place to hang the washing by stringing lines across the garden; fetching washing baskets to hang it up; and building a little house near by with screens and muslins to extend the 'home' play, which could (and has in my kindergarten) led to all the children becoming involved in the process of doing the washing, hanging it up, making ironing boards out of planks with wooden blocks as irons, dressing the dolls, cooking the dinner, and generally involving all and sundry in household activities.

Around or after the age of five the play begins to change. Many children experience what could be called 'boredom' at this age. They often say 'I don't know what to do'. It is as if they have been abandoned by their imagination and fantasy, and have no ideas left. This is the time where they can be stimulated directly by the adult work. They should be encouraged to join in with the work in the kindergarten, cutting up the vegetables or fruit, having tasks such as sewing, weaving or woodwork – always tasks which need to be completed. It does not take long for this phase to pass. It could be hours or a few days before new ideas for play arise naturally, and the transformation from one type of play to another takes place.

Now the initial idea comes first, followed by the attempt to find the right materials. They have a mental image of what they want to do or be. For instance, before the age of five, the child sees a stick, picks it up and begins to play at being a knight, with the stick as a sword. After roughly the age of five they say, 'I would like to be a knight, and I need a sword'. Then they look around for wood to make one, and generally it needs to look right! They have a mental image of what the sword should look like, and could spend hours sawing, hammering and sanding this sword until it looks good enough to play with. The impulse changes from being stimulated by the object or toy which leads them to the play, to the idea for the play, then looking for the toy or object to support it. The imagination is set to work again!

Older children's play

Readiness for more formal education is a measure of a child's abilities as a whole developing human being: what Steiner referred to when he spoke about the threefoldness of the human being. One-sided development can only leave other sides undeveloped. Only when a child is . . .

- physically/bodily ready (ideally, robust, coordinated, secure);
- mentally ready (ideally, able to begin to think in self-generated mental pictures and sequences);
- socially and linguistically ready (ideally, able to learn in a group, and to communicate needs);
- spiritually ready (ideally, able to begin to learn out of authority)

. . . can we really speak of readiness for formal education. In most cases, children are not ready in this holistic sense before they are 6 years old. Therefore they spend this last year in the kindergarten, working on developing skills needed for the next stage.

During this last year in the kindergarten, the educators work more with the will forces of the child. It is important that the children complete the tasks that they begin, that they begin to take responsibility for themselves, their actions, and for others. The children have tasks which contribute to the well-being of themselves and of others, and of the world around them. They tidy, clean, sweep, decorate, cook, take care of plants and animals, serve others, run messages, help the 'little ones' and develop skills and coordination which will help them later on. Their craft work takes on a different dimension. They may complete a 'handwork bag' for big school, design and sew it. They may make their own knotted doll and weave a blanket to wrap it in, or make a wooden puppet or boat. All of these skills develop hand-eye coordination, small and large motor skills, concentration, and an ability to follow and understand instructions. They can transform the mental image which arises through words into their own activity.

During play, the children now need clearly defined limits and clear directions, such as 'we don't shoot each other in our kindergarten', or 'that play is not suitable for inside, please wait until we go outside'. This sets limits and boundaries for the child, which are quite suitable to their age. Further directions can also be given now to extend their play, such as, 'why don't you fetch some paper and a stick and make a flag for the top of your castle?' Here is an example from my kindergarten: some children had built a boat. The older boys were beginning to get a bit rowdy, and the younger children who were passengers and sitting quietly fishing from the side, became upset at the noise. I suggested to one of them that they may need a basket to collect the fish from the fishermen. This led to some rope-making (twisting wool together to make ropes), and then the children built an extensive contraption with the ropes and some baskets, using hoists and levers, poles and planks to wind the baskets out of the water. This extended play not only lasted at least an hour that morning, but throughout the rest of the week, changing and growing all the time.

Sally Jenkinson puts it very aptly:

> There are precious few places where children can freely develop their own culture, and where the creative spirit of childhood can perform its magical transformations . . . A Steiner Waldorf Kindergarten tries to be such a place; a place where the echoing voices of children at play can still be heard.
>
> (Jenkinson 2006:6)

Figure 4.2 Houses

Play today

It can no longer be taken for granted that all children can play with spontaneity, fulfilment and enthusiasm appropriate for their stage of development. This is owing to the influences to which they are subjected; for example, electronic gadgetry, TV, the media and ready-made technically sophisticated toys, which leave behind a feeling of emptiness and a demand for more. Saturation entertainment has taken over the playtime and home life of children.

Sally Jenkinson gives the following example:

> A mother once told me how her child had once played a game of postman. The slatted back of a dining chair became his post box; he made his own letters and tiny stamps (complete with queen's head), borrowed a hat and cloak, made himself a silver foil badge and played at delivering letters to various destinations around his house for hours. A kind aunt, having seen his obvious delight in the game while visiting, later bought him a manufactured toy postman

set from the shops. He never played with it. The charm of his own play lay in his creative participation and in his ability to transform; each little invention brought its own pleasure and allowed the child to add something of himself to the game.

(Jenkinson 2001:121)

The time for play, as you will see in Chapter 6, is given a large part of the kindergarten morning. The 'empty' space into which the children come (inside or out), leaves huge scope for the child's creativity and imagination. There is enormous freedom for their play – nothing is previously set up, no hospitals, post offices or hairdressers, no intentions for the children's learning, no teacher planning or preparation – just an empty space provided: an atmosphere of industry and calm and simple toys, natural materials and playthings provided should the children need them.

Toys and playthings

Play is stimulated by external circumstances, so objects the children play with should not be complete and should be able to be transformed by them

Visitors to a Steiner kindergarten are always surprised at what they see as a 'lack' of playthings for the children. There are certain considerations, however, which are taken into account when choosing toys for the children:

- They stimulate the imagination and fantasy by being whatever the child wants them to be.
- They appeal to the senses, by being made from natural materials in soft colours.
- They are 'collectable' from nature; e.g. sea shells, pebbles, pine cones.
- They enable the children to create anew each time; a fresh invention.
- They are not electronic or programmable.
- They are repairable where possible.
- They can be home-made.

Figure 4.3 Home corner

- They represent items found in the home or outdoors.
- They are as simple and beautiful as possible.

Some suggested toys in the kindergarten

- **Baskets** containing: pine cones (trees for floor play or puppet shows, food or kindling for a pretend fire); pebbles of all sizes (for sorting, making patterns, floor play or food); conkers; clothes pegs; bark; feathers; shaped wood for building bricks; wool (for tying, rope-making, weaving); carded or washed and dyed sheep's wool in different colours; play-cloths such as lengths (half metre to metres) of dyed muslin, silk, cotton, wool (for making walls, houses, dressing up, wrapping dolls), bean bags, etc.
- **Building:** Wooden planks of different lengths with slightly rounded corners; large logs cut into slices and large building blocks; low

boxes and stools, carpets, mats and tables for building on; clothes stands (fold-out, such as old washing stands, or purpose-built to act as houses, shops, puppet theatres).

- **Dressing-up clothes:** Different materials to act as saris, dresses, fairy wings, cloaks, crowns, hats, scarves, bags.

- **Home corner:** Containing tables and stools/chairs, kitchen equipment (cooker, etc.), scoops, baskets, crockery and cutlery, dolls beds or hammocks, including bedding, cushions, lengths of material, baskets for shopping, etc.

- **Hobby horses, prams:** The older children sometimes make and ride hobby horses, and are often seen pushing the dolls in their prams.

- **Dolls:** The doll is considered one of the most important toys for children of all ages. It is the image of a human being and is therefore important for developing the self-image of the child. In the kindergarten dolls are not complete in all anatomical details, nor technically perfect, but made in such a way as to enable the children to use their imagination so that the doll can embody every possible view of the human being.

  - The **knotted doll** is the first; one which many children make for themselves in their last year of kindergarten. It is simply made by knotting a piece of flannelette into head and arms, leaving the rest loose, then hemmed. The eyes and mouth are simply marked with a crayon.

  - The **formed doll** is the most common doll used in the kindergarten, and this too is made simply from fleece-stuffed fabric, is soft and cuddly, with woollen hair which can be plaited or tied up, and eyes and mouth sewn in a neutral expression. The child can imagine the smile, the frown, the tears or the joy according to its mood. They are able to be dressed, swaddled, taken for rides in the pram, put to bed, 'fed' or cared for as a parent would their own child.

- **For floor or tabletop play:** Small, wooden, simply formed animals; families that are able to stand, puppets; knitted or sewn animals; carts, boats; curved wood used for houses or bridges; houses carved from logs; wheeled toys such as trains made from small logs or carved wood cars.

- **Outside toys:** Consist of large building materials, sticks and branches, logs and planks (for making see-saws or slides, tents and tepees), collections of shells, pebbles, etc., as before. Digging equipment is important for gardening or sandpit play. Rope ladders, climbing equipment, tyres, trees, bricks and ropes for building, hoops and skipping ropes, stilts and horse harnesses, and some rolling equipment, such as wooden carts, wheelbarrows, and so on. We do not use bikes or scooters as they cannot be used imaginatively for construction.

Figure 4.4 Floor play

The kindergarten environment

The entrance lobby

The entrance to the kindergarten room is warm, welcoming and parent-friendly. You will find child-height coat pegs, a bench under which there is a shelf for slippers, shoes and Wellington boots (unless they are kept in a separate place near the outside door with the wet-weather gear). There is usually a parents' notice board, indications of what is happening in the kindergarten that week, a diary and some photographs. The festivals and events are often displayed outside the room as well. There is often a library and school shop, fresh flowers and seasonal display, as well as a parents' helping rota (parents are expected to participate in the life of the kindergarten, including the cleaning, washing-up and occasionally taking the washing home).

The kindergarten room

This should be a warm, welcoming and artistically decorated space, which serves as the setting for what the day's impulse brings. Many kindergartens, where possible, have the kitchen area integral to the room. This usually contains a cooker, kettle, toaster, sink and washing and preparing facilities. The kitchen area is separated from the main room by the work surface and a small gate which prevents access to the children. They can stand on a special box step on the outside of the preparation work area and reach the sink. Furniture is small–scale and child-friendly, and near to the kitchen are the tables and chairs for activities. These are all made of wood. There is a home-play corner, a quiet area (in some

Figure 5.1 The kindergarten

cases, with a few select picture books), and a large, empty play area with carpet (big enough for the ring-time circle). Shelves and baskets contain equipment and cloths, and there are usually a few clothes stands for building houses.

The room is painted (usually colour-washed) in a pale pink (Rudolf Steiner described it as 'peach-blossom pink') and is sometimes decorated with seasonal branches, crafts and mobiles. Corners are sometimes softened with hanging muslins as well. The windows are curtained with pink-dyed muslins, and the electric lighting, if used at all, is subdued. Sometimes there will be pictures on the walls representing the family: father, mother and child, or groups of children. The whole impression is of a calm, uncluttered and peaceful environment.

There are no displays of children's work on the walls, although at times, if the children have been busy with a seasonal craft, this will be hanging in some area of the room: spider web weaving; birds at Whitsun; Valentine hearts; tissue-paper butterflies; felted chicks. All of these add to the seasonal feel of the room, and are taken home at the appropriate time.

Figure 5.2 Seasonal table at Harvest

The seasonal table

This is placed in a position within the room where it is visible and central, and yet unobtrusive. The seasonal table is a place where treasures are displayed and woven together with elements of the season's mood. It develops and changes throughout the year to reflect the changing festivals or seasons.

The colours are dictated by the colours in the environment at the time of year, or of the festival. Dyed muslins or silk veils are arranged loosely as the background and table cloth. The colours in the summer would be a sunny yellow sky and a light green cloth for the earth. In winter, it would be a snowy white and pale blue sky. At Christmas there would be a deep blue sky with stars, and green and brown cloths on the table. At Diwali the colours would be red and gold, and so on.

The four elements are also usually included in some way: earth (stones and crystals), water (could be a bowl, or a blue silk cloth), fire (a candle for lighting at special times), and air (a mobile, which also tends to change seasonally), as well as man or animal (people, gnomes, fairies, ducks, and other animals).

The children do not play with the scene, as it is created specially by the teacher, but are encouraged to look out for special seasonal 'gifts' to bring: shells, crystals, pine cones, conkers, apples and berries, and always fresh seasonal flowers.

The outside environment

The outside environment should be as 'natural' as possible. Facilities will (premises permitting) include a sandpit, a digging area, trees to climb, a fire pit, a compost area, fruit trees and an organic vegetable garden. Flowers are grown throughout the year for bringing inside for the seasonal and eating table. Occasionally you will find purpose-built climbing equipment and swings, if space allows. There is usually a hut of some kind where the children can escape to when it rains or can play in, such as a Wendy house. The children, if fortunate enough, can build a willow hut or tunnel with a teacher or parent, and occasionally you will find a bread oven where bread can be cooked and eaten outside.

The parents often join the teachers and children at work in the garden, which helps to create a good community spirit.

A move to forest (woodland) kindergartens has begun in some settings, and two or more days a week may be spent entirely outdoors in the woods or fields. All activities happen in the woodland environment: tents may be constructed in rainy weather and crafts can be made from natural materials found by the children. Ring time, story and lunch will all take place outdoors, and the rhythm of the kindergarten day followed. The outdoor provision differs from the norm of 'forest schools' in that what takes place is not geared to extend learning, but rather to extend experience; to become one with nature; to enliven the senses; and experience awe and wonder for the natural environment, the elements, the seasons and the weather. Sitting around a fire which is heating soup for lunch, after a long walk through snow and ice, is an experience to be remembered, as is weaving buttercup or daisy chains while lying in long grass on a warm summer's day.

Figure 5.3 Outside environment

After a recent visit to the UK by the Danish pedagogue Helle Heckmann, there has been a move to take long walks each morning with the children. She promotes 'slow education': a slowing down of the rhythm of the day to counterbalance the haste and stress of modern life. She suggests that for children to balance their physical movements today and to build stamina, there is a need for rhythmic walking. A twenty-minute walk around the local community, or to a park, engages children with the community happenings: the postman delivering letters; dogs in a garden; crossing the road to the shop; or chatting to neighbours. Singing while they walk, or chatting to each other builds verbal skills, and stopping to listen to a bird sing, or a car coming around the corner, enlivens the senses. Returning back to the setting, the children are ready for a drink or snack, and can share experiences of the morning walk.

6 | Rhythm, repetition and reverence

Often referred to as the three 'Rs' of Steiner Waldorf early childhood, these key themes underpin the kindergarten practice and are important educational principles. They give structure and form to the child's daily life and enable them to feel secure, safe, to know where they are in the world. Children need the reassurance of continuity, and regular events mark the kindergarten day, week and year.

Rhythm

In the *Oxford English Dictionary*, 'rhythm' is defined as:

- a measured flow of words or phrases in verse or prose determined by various relations of long or short or accented and unaccented syllables;
- music accented or duration of notes;
- physiological movement with a regular succession of strong or weak elements (heart/pulse);
- a regularly recurring sequence of events;
- (art) a harmonious correlation of parts.

Rhythm is the regular recurrence of an event which goes through a cycle within a space or time. There are many different rhythms which dominate our lives. For example:

- The daily rhythm of day and night (and within it of eating, getting up and going to sleep, and the small rhythms within this, such as brushing teeth and washing hands).

- The rhythm of the seasons through a cycle within the year.

- Festivals and celebrations which occur regularly throughout our lives, such as birthdays and religious and cultural festivals such as Christmas and Diwali.

- Rhythms also mediate between polar activities, birth and death, rest and movement and so on. They clearly have a quality of orderliness.

In the body, we are also governed by rhythm, predominantly the rhythm of the heart (heartbeat) and the breathing rhythm of inhalation and exhalation, which occurs unconsciously for the most part. These and many other rhythms govern our lives.

Before birth

Rhythm begins before birth, for there is rhythm already in the womb. It is the mother's rhythm which governs the embryo, and later, the growing foetus picks up both their own and their mother's rhythms of sound, such as the heart beating or the blood pumping.

After birth

After birth we have to establish our own rhythm but the baby needs help from their mother, otherwise the mother (and the baby) will be driven to distraction of not knowing what will happen when. This begins the establishment of regular habits, such as feeding, sleep, activity.

Toddlers

For the toddler, rhythms are usually established through daily activities and in the routine of the week, such as washing day, shopping day, parent and child group day, baking day, cleaning day. They become aware of the rhythm of singing, rhyming, swinging, washing, sweeping, polishing, etc. They are settled and reassured by the routines still supported by the care-taker (parent, childminder and others). They become more consciously aware of the changing seasons, of celebrations and festivals, of daily events. They are reassured by this for it begins to give a structure to their life.

The daily rhythm in the kindergarten

There is a varied pace to the rhythmical structure of the day; periods of contraction and expansion which provide a balance between times of activity and times of rest. This might mean that creative play could be followed by a painting activity, or energetic outdoor play by a quiet puppet show. There is a rhythmic alternation between the child's time (creative play, outside time) and the teacher's time (ring time, story): the teacher's time being comparatively short at this age. Working with rhythm helps children to live with change, to find their place in the world, and to begin to understand the past, present and future. It provides a very real foundation for the understanding of time – what has gone before and what will follow – and helps children to relate to the natural and the human world. Attention to rhythm promotes healthy development and leads to a balanced life later. Rhythm helps to harmonise the early will forces (which drive the young child into constant activity) and to stabilise their feeling life.

Rhythm in the kindergarten is a swinging activity between contraction and expansion; we need both to become balanced. If there is too much breathing in, (contraction) we have a tendency to become quiet, retiring, inward, antisocial, anxious and physically cold. However, if there is too much breathing out (expansion) we can become sociable, relaxed and warm, or in extremes, overstimulated and hyperactive. Nevertheless, all natural breathing is done unconsciously in a relaxed way and this is also the case in the kindergarten, where the child is unaware of the rhythmic structure in place, but settles happily into it.

So rhythm is used within the day to aid this healthy development of the child's rhythmic system and also as a tool to make life easier for teachers and parents. There is a structure to the day which allows little space for chaos (although we are not absolutely static or rigid in this). If the teacher is unprepared and there are gaps in the rhythmic flow of the day, we really feel it! It allows space for anything to happen.

At this age, space and time mean little to the child: for instance, if the young child asks what time it is, they do not want to know literally; they want to know if it is time for tea (they are hungry) or time for bed (they are sleepy, although they usually deny this while yawning all the time). The child is the centre of their universe, and whatever happens around them needs to relate directly to their needs.

The teacher is the centre of the kindergarten and therefore must be well-prepared to build up the rhythm creatively. And at home rhythm is the perfect aid to easier parenting. If the child *always* goes to bed at 7 p.m. then they will start yawning at that time and will usually go to bed without a fuss (until they are 10 years old if you are lucky! My daughter regularly, at exactly 8.30 p.m., used to say 'I'm not tired', while yawning profusely).

The child's rhythms are already broken by staggered kindergarten sessions (for those children who only attend two or three days a week) and the break at weekends. Therefore what is offered is the rhythm within the morning, the rhythm of the week (Monday, baking; Tuesday, painting; Wednesday, crafts; Thursday, cooking; Friday, gardening and cleaning), and the rhythm of the seasons, the rhythm of the year, which provide stability in an ever-changing social and family life.

The child becomes confident, strong and secure, moving freely and orientating easily within the form and structure of the kindergarten. The world becomes familiar and the child feels safe.

Repetition

In the *Oxford English Dictionary*, 'repetition' is defined as:

- The act or instance of repeating or being repeated;
- The thing repeated;

- A piece to be learned by heart;
- The ability of a musical instrument or voice to repeat a note;
- To say something out loud, to do something again, to say aloud something heard;
- To aid memory/or repeat without thinking (repeat parrot fashion).

Repetition plays a key role in establishing continuity and in the healthy development of memory. Children's memories are strengthened by recurring experiences, and daily, weekly and yearly events in kindergarten are remembered and often eagerly anticipated a second time around. Stories are told not just once, but many times. Repetition brings the opportunity for children to familiarise themselves with the material and to deepen their relationship with it.

Repetition is a general aid to learning and memory, and when we repeat something often enough it becomes a habit. Repetition strengthens and educates the will forces of the child; it takes will to repeat tasks. Repetition occurs not only daily (the daily routine), but weekly in daily activities (as above), which are repeated on the same days throughout the year, and yearly in the repeated seasonal activities, festivals and celebrations. This again gives the children security and stability within the familiar.

Rhythm and repetition in the kindergarten day

A typical day is described in the following section. However, this may differ from one setting to another. There is a move, as described above, to begin in the garden, to start with a long walk, or to meet in the forest and spend the entire day outdoors. If this happens, a rhythm similar to the one below is still followed where possible. You will also see that it is a combination of teacher-led and child-initiated activity, and that even within the teacher-led session, there is freedom for the individual child to take part by their own initiative, or to be drawn into the activity by imitating the adults or their peers.

The kindergarten staff often meet in the morning to say a verse together, prepare materials and bring the right mood into the room before the children's arrival. The children are brought into the kindergarten by their parent or carer. They leave the outside behind by taking off shoes and hanging up coats before being brought into the main room and handed over to the care of the teacher, who greets each child in turn. (There is often a moment for a quick word between parent and teacher if required.) Many children no longer have the rhythmical walk to school, and usually come in somewhat stressed from the car journey, or from being 'hurried' to school. (How often do parents catch themselves saying 'hurry up, we'll be late'?) The children are drawn to join the activity of the teacher and assistant, who are usually involved in the daily preparation of the snack or other activity at this time. Cooking, drawing, sewing, woodwork or weaving are possibilities until they have relaxed enough to join or begin the play.

Creative play can be seen as an expansion; a breathing out within the kindergarten room. The children now have freedom (within the structure) to develop their own play constructively. The teachers interfere as little as possible, but are there to guide the play if necessary. As mentioned in Chapter 3, the role of the teacher is a different one here, for they are doing adult work such as sewing, mending or helping where required; they interrupt play only to guide the children through various social situations if necessary. (They also use this time to observe the children carefully, which is recorded later.) During this time the children re-enact what they have observed in the outside world, learning negotiating skills, caring and sharing, establishing societies and social interaction, which are all aids to future good citizenship. The kindergarten is a community where each member has an important contribution to make.

The **daily activity** may then take place, and for some of these activities the children come together to the tables as a group. At other times, some may be drawn to the activity while others play. These activities include baking, modelling beeswax, a seasonal craft, or painting and drawing. Coming together for activities like these creates a particularly peaceful, creative mood. The children sit at the table and the activities are introduced with songs and finger rhymes which are suitable for the activity taking place. The activities help the children to gain control and mobility of their fingers and learn new skills.

Before continuing with the day, the play materials and activities need to be tidied away, and in many kindergartens, the children and teacher

Figure 6.1 Baking

come together and refuel a little by eating a few raisins or sunflower seeds (always a good opportunity for counting), and in some cases have a chat to the tidy gnome puppet. This calling to the circle happens through singing. So the teacher would sing using a lullaby tune, 'everybody come to the circle . . . everybody come and sit by me', and repeat this until all the children have gathered quietly on the carpet. The children do this in a dreamy way, and hardly ever react with 'I'm not finished playing yet!'. Repetition of the same song and the daily rhythm help. After the mini-snack, finger game or gentle conversation, either with a puppet or directly with the teacher and their friends, the children, out of imitation of the teacher and assistant, begin to tidy the playthings away, again with a song.

> I met a little dusty gnome, he said it's time to clean our room,
>
> Round, round, round, whish, whish, whish, clean our room.
>
> (Wynstones Collection: *Spindrift*)

Or,

> Tidy time, it's tidy time, let us tidy up today
>
> Let us put it all away . . . It's tidy time . . .
>
> (Author's own rhyme)

Figure 6.2 Tidy time

The teachers and children **tidy up** properly, putting each item into its correct basket, container, house or shop. Tidying becomes an activity and not a chore, and caring for the environment is always an important consideration. Sorting and counting, folding and rolling cloths, matching items and dressing dolls; all this is important to get the room ready for play the next day.

During the tidy time the children also set the table for the snack. It is usually the older children who are given this task, but often if a younger child wishes to help they do so out of imitation of the older children. Here is another opportunity for counting: laying the table with the right number of cups and plates, chairs and spoons. The table is always beautifully decorated with flowers, a candle and sometimes even a display of animals, little figures, or seasonal objects in the centre.

Ring time comes next. This contains both rhythm and repetition. Now is the opportunity for expansion and contraction within the circle, with the teacher as the focus. Gesture, movement and speech must be clear, precise, beautiful and meaningful: worthy of imitation. During ring time, which is repeated over two or even three weeks, the children have the opportunity to learn other languages and trace the seasons, or act out the stories which have been told. The children learn through repetition and this aids their memory. It is within ring time that many of the pre-literacy skills which will be needed for later, more formal literacy are developed, such as listening, rhyme, letter sounds, alphabet, counting, rhythms in music (pulse and beat), and interacting with each other in the circle games played. Ring time is usually seasonal and by repeating them the children 'absorb' an enormous store of the rhymes and songs which are contained in it. There is movement which helps physical development, and large and small motor skills are used, from finger games to balancing, jumping, hopping and skipping, as well as being aware of each other in space. Ring time begins and ends with a verse to greet each other and the new day.

> Good morning, dear earth, and good morning, dear sun.
> Good morning, dear stones and flowers, everyone.
> Good morning, dear animals, and birds on the tree.
> Good morning to you, and good morning to me.
> (Wynstones Collection: Gateways)

And it can end:

> Two little hands, as dirty as can be,
> That's because they have been baking (drawing, painting, etc.),
>   you see.
> So we must wash them, and make a wee . . .
> (Author's own rhyme)

From ring time a long line of children lead to the **toilet**, singing all the way. Getting the children to go to go to the toilet or wash hands is never a problem; it is a rhythm ingrained through constant repetition. They simply can't eat until their hands are clean! As there is no

Figure 6.3 Ring time

questioning them as to whether they need to go or not: there is no argument.

The children come together again for **snack time**. This is an opportunity for social interaction, to nourish the physical body, to listen and be heard. The serviettes are given out, often by an older child, matching name to child. The meal starts with a blessing on the food, lighting a candle as a focus for thanksgiving, and saying thank you for the meal together when it is finished. (Even the youngest children will sit at the table for over half an hour without fidgeting. They all do it!)

> Blessings on the blossom and blessings on the fruit,
> And blessings on the leaf and stem, and blessings on the root.
> And blessings on our meal.
>
> (Wynstones Collection: *Spindrift*)

The children's physical development is nourished and supported through the largely organic food which they receive in the kindergarten.

The new or younger children are fussy at first, but soon eat even the crustiest bread, salad from the garden, apple skins, muesli and vegetable soup (for they see the other children doing it and imitation is a powerful stimulus). Nothing is wasted; what is left goes out for the birds or compost. When everyone has finished, the group once again holds hands and says 'thank you' for the meal. The candle is snuffed out and the children take their cups and plates to the kitchen area. Once again, some older children remain for a while to help with the cleaning while the others get ready to go outside.

Garden time comes next, and everyone goes outside. It is important that the children are able to experience all the extremes of the weather, and they are expected to be properly dressed in waterproof clothing, hats and gloves in the winter, and sunhats and sleeves in the summer. This is a perfect opportunity for them to learn to tie laces, do up zips and buttons and, when they have managed it themselves, to help the younger children. Quite a lot of time is allowed for this. Wellington boots are worn most of the time as the play tends to get rather muddy, and they do a great deal of digging! Now the children are expected to be *doing*, actively experiencing their physical bodies and the space around them. Young children do not have a good awareness of space (noticeable by the way they often bump into things or each other, or trip over steps or objects), so the teachers and children work on this by throwing balls, playing ring games, skipping with ropes (big and small), balancing, climbing, gardening and strengthening the limbs. These all help the children to become confident in their bodies and develop new skills. Sometimes the children are taken on walks to the park, and they learn road awareness and listening skills too. In most kindergartens the children tend an organic vegetable garden. They dig the ground over, plant the seeds, water, weed, and eventually harvest the fruit and vegetables for eating. Digging up potatoes is a favourite. Finding worms to break up the soil, hunting ladybirds and caterpillars, feeding the birds and hedgehogs, caring for the pond so that they can watch the frogs and toads spawn and the tadpoles grow, gives much joy. There is always a sandpit, a gravel or mud pit for 'digging to Australia' and trees to climb (with the appropriate risk assessments, of course). The children have access to large planks and sticks for building tents and tepees, rocks and bricks for walls, spades, forks and rakes for digging, and water. The teacher and assistant work alongside the children in the garden, always occupied and observing everything.

The children return to the kindergarten room for **story time**. After washing hands and changing into indoor clothes, they gather together in a circle, sit quietly and listen to a story told (not read) by the teacher. This is an opportunity for the children to completely 'switch off' physically and enter a dream world of fantasy and imagination, where they can build pictures inwardly. Here, stories learned by heart are told to the children, or puppet shows are performed, repeating them sometimes for a week or more until they become a friend and a companion. Stories are chosen carefully (folk, nature or fairy tales) and the vocabulary is vast. The fairy tales carry deep moral truths within them and set before the children a picture of how the human being can develop itself to do a task worthy of mankind. Puppet shows, sometimes the showing of beautiful books with moving pictures, and plays, enhance the children's understanding of stories. Children whose first language is not English are given extra help where necessary by giving a copy of the story, and sometimes a translation, to the parent to read to the child at home. The repeated nature of the storytelling supports their acquisition of English.

After the story has finished, we sing a goodbye song:

Goodbye to you, goodbye to you, we'll see you soon again.
It's time to go so don't be late, we'll wave goodbye at the garden gate.
Goodbye to you, goodbye to you, we'll see you soon again.

(Author's own rhyme)

A quiet game is often played until all those going home have been collected. The children who remain for afternoon care make up a little bed with mattress, blanket and pillow, and lie down for a rest before the afternoon session. The parents are encouraged to continue the rhythm at home, and are reminded that the children have been working hard at play all morning, for this is children's 'work', and the afternoon needs to be peaceful with lots of outside play, or going for a walk, for walking has its own rhythm. Hyperactivity can be a result of lack of activity, and

Figure 6.4 Puppet story

walking is a rhythmic healthy activity. Parents are encouraged not to fill the afternoons with further activities as the children need to absorb the experiences of the morning without further stimulation.

Another way in which rhythm and repetition is brought into the day is through singing. **Singing** is a subtle way of penetrating the consciousness of children without awakening them too much. It is gentle and repetitive and the songs used are very, very simple. Calling songs tend to be in minor third and fifth chords. If you call 'coo-ee' to your neighbour across the garden, you usually do this in a dropped minor third (top D down to B; or top D down to B and G (5th) on the piano).

Singing contains both rhythm and repetition. When you sing, you cannot really be angry or upset. We use singing in the kindergarten to 'break through' situations, call children to attention, calm things down, communicate and give instructions. And we sing with joy! Our feeling life (emotion) is involved with the rhythmic system. Music is emotionally involving. Often when we listen to music, our breathing imitates it. Singing used in the right way can be calming. However, we don't sing all the time, as then it would just become background noise, and the children would 'switch it off'.

Reverence

Reverence for the child

Rudolf Steiner asked the teachers to 'receive each child with reverence' and look not only at the physical body of the child, but also at the spirit and soul. These qualities all make up the human being, and all need nurturing. He asked teachers to see the child coming towards them from a spiritual world, and this image is uniquely portrayed in an extract of a poem, 'Ode: Intimations of Immortality', by William Wordsworth.

> Our birth is but a sleep and a forgetting;
> The Soul that rises with us, our life's Star
> Hath had elsewhere its setting,
> And cometh from afar;
> Not in entire forgetfulness,
> And not in utter nakedness
> But trailing clouds of glory do we come
> From God, who is our home:
> Heaven lies about us in our infancy!

In some kindergartens hangs a framed print of Raphael's *Sistine Madonna*. This is another representation of the child, surrounded by angels and held with love in the arms of his mother. Children are comforted by this unconsciously, and some teachers use it as a form of meditative study: 'Where has the child come from, where are they going, and what can I do to support them?'

The picture of the child as a threefold being enables the teacher to see each as more than the physical body standing before them; as bearing a bag of gifts which the teacher can help them to unwrap. Enhancing and developing those gifts is our task with each child. This was once described to me by my mother, Estelle Bryer, a therapist, teacher and author, who wrote a letter to her nine-year-old granddaughter, who was concerned that she was not doing well at a school subject:

> Every person is born with a bag of gifts. Some never even open their bags, and their unused gifts vanish. Others work hard at opening their gifts and using them wisely, and when one is worked with properly, another always appears. Other gifts are only ready to be found in later life. The most important thing is to have a golden heart . . . that is given to many as a gift but we have to work hard at polishing it with good deeds so that it can always shine . . . it makes our eyes sparkle!

In the kindergarten day there are moments of reverence, and the teachers lovingly create opportunities for the children to experience joy, awe and wonder. Wonder is a reverential experience, enabling the children to experience life itself in all its beauty. To create that 'ah' moment at any opportunity, brings a sense of peace and joy to the child's learning about life's eternal possibilities.

These reverential moments are also awakened during the celebrations and festivals, both cultural and religious, and the celebration of the child's birthday is one which both the parent and child remember forever.

A child's birthday in a kindergarten

The celebration of a child's birthday is performed a little differently by each teacher. Below is one way of doing it.

Before the child comes into the classroom on either the morning of the birthday, or soon afterwards (never before), the teacher has prepared a birthday table, decorated with a special cloth, flowers, a birthday candle, a birthday crown, space for a cake brought from home, a card with a drawing for the child (done by the teacher) with a birthday poem which, in some way, draws on the child's gifts, and a small present made by the teacher. In my kindergarten we had different gifts for each age: a finger

Figure 6.5 Birthday celebration

puppet bird for those turning four; a bean bag with ribbons (for throwing) for those turning five; and always something special for the six year olds, such as a special wooden whistle, a boat or a handmade figure for playing with. Prior to the day, the parent had provided the teacher with a 'potted history' of special events marking the child's development.

The parent has the opportunity to spend the morning with the child, and accompanies the child to kindergarten. During the first part of the morning, the children draw a card for the birthday child, or a birthday book is made from the drawings of all the children. This is placed on the birthday table as well, and when it is time for ring time, the children and teacher form a ring, say the verse as normal, and then hold hands singing a special song for the child:

Today is a happy, happy, happy day . . . today is a happy day,
And why is it a happy, happy, happy day . . . and why is it a happy day?
Because it's Debbie's happy birthday, it's Debbie's happy birthday.
(Author's own rhyme)

The parent then sits in the centre of the ring of children, while the birthday child and their chosen friend (their *angel*) go to the outside of the ring. The angel is given wings and a star crown to wear. The teacher ceremoniously lights the birthday candle and gives it to the parent, who is sitting in the centre of the circle. Then the birthday child, led by their angel, weaves in and out of the children standing in the circle, while they sing this song:

> In heaven shines a golden star, an angel brought me from afar.
> From heaven high unto the earth, and brought me to my house of
> birth.
>
> (Wynstones Collection: Gateways)

The angel brings the child to their parent who hands them the 'light of life', and they carefully carry the candle to the birthday table. (This is a moment of such joy and wonder, that most parents are quite overcome with emotion.) Then it is time to put on the birthday crown and look at the presents and cards. The birthday candle is put in a safe place until the meal.

During snack time, once all the children are sitting and all is quiet, the birthday candle is brought to the table and the children hear the developmental story. This begins with the little angel journeying from heaven, having collected gifts for her future life on earth from the sun, moon and stars. She crosses the rainbow bridge and is born into the arms of her new family. Thereafter follow the milestones and rather fun achievements which the parent has given to the teacher, which are woven into a story of the child to date. With each birthday, a candle is lit on the cake, and when all are lit, the traditional 'Happy Birthday' song is sung, and the candles are blown out. At the end of the day, the child takes everything home.

Reverence for each other

In facilitating the personal, social and moral development of the children, the teachers endeavour to be a role model worthy of imitation, and make sure that their relationships with the parents, children and their colleagues are respectful, caring, empathetic and warm. The children hopefully imitate this and, through their creative play and daily social activities, learn to interact positively with each other. In kindergarten they are encouraged to share, work together and cooperate with each other, also establishing effective relationships with their teachers and other adults.

The older children who are already familiar with kindergarten increasingly assume the role of helpers. They look after the younger children, which is particularly important for children who grow up with older brothers and sisters. Working with the social will forces of the six year olds by both modelling and encouraging the attitude of caring for, listening to and helping others, provide the child with a basis for more conscious empathy and social awareness in later years. And if practised enough it develops into unconscious good habits.

Reverence for the environment

The environment and environmental issues are important for the well-being and the future of our earth, and in the kindergarten emphasis is placed on caring for the physical surroundings, inside and outside. The kindergarten needs to be cared for, as do its contents. The toys, being mostly wood are easily polished and mended, unlike plastic toys which generally have to be thrown away when broken. Buttons and torn clothing are sewn and washed (dolls, children's and fabrics used by the children), the kindergarten is cleaned as a weekly activity (polished, swept daily and the floors, walls equipment and windows washed), all with the children. The garden is cared for, the birds fed with breadcrumbs, the compost tended and everything recycled, which introduces children to the idea of ecology and forms an important part of the curriculum. Nothing is wasted.

Reverence for food

Nature is thanked for providing the children with good food to eat (see verse above). Where possible, it is grown in the garden and tended

Figure 6.6 Snack time

with care. It is harvested, cooked and enjoyed by all. Food can also be brought from home, and shared together in soup or as fruit salad, prepared during the morning with the children's help. The children sit at the table and eat in a social way until all have finished. The older children take turns in serving the bread or fruit, taking it round to the others at the table and pouring their drinks. 'Thank you' is commonly heard.

There is a focus today on the diet of children with so many that are malnourished or obese. Providing a well-balanced diet is essential, as is encouraging the children to eat a wide variety of foods: chopped, grated, raw, cooked, savoury or sweet, hot or cold. Preparing the food together makes it more acceptable to try it together. Encouraging words such as 'strong teeth are good for crunching carrots', or turning the process into a story where the rabbit 'loved the sweet taste of the delicious purple sprouting broccoli', or 'the tortoise chewed the lettuce 'just like that', then demonstrating these for the children, are helpful examples. Having the same foods on the same days of the week also helps them to get into a rhythm, and they become familiar with them over a period of time. Although porridge day is a Tuesday, it can be served with honey and lemon, cinnamon and butter, apple and raisin; each week a different way. Bread can be served with savoury spreads or jams, and the fruit or vegetables can be beautifully arranged in patterns on the plates to be passed around. Nourishment comes not only from the food but also from the smell, taste and the way it is presented. Respecting the food means we also respect what becomes of it when we have finished. Recycling it, either to birds, animals or the compost heap, is essential in learning how to care for the environment and for the future of our planet!

7 | The celebration of festivals

Festivals and celebrations mark the passing of time. They are fondly remembered throughout our lives as significant 'happenings', be they seasonal, cultural or celebrations, such as birthdays and christenings, bar mitzvahs, anniversaries, or even funerals.

Celebrating festivals with children helps to establish continuity – the rhythm and repetition– which give form and structure to their lives. These two elements, as well as reverence, are significantly present in all festivals and celebrations.

Figure 7.1 May festival

To celebrate a festival with children we have to be active in it, as children learn by being active in their will, their doing. Festivals need to be a complete artistic experience, to appeal to all the senses and we need to consider all the things which make up a festival:

- history, meaning and purpose
- food
- costumes
- music
- mood (colour)
- story/puppet play.

Religious, cultural and seasonal festivals

In the spring and summer, there are fewer festivals than in the autumn and winter. The summer festivals are significant in their outwardness: reaching out to humanity in a gesture of sacrifice and rebirth (spring/ Easter); brotherhood and community (Whitsun); and reaching out to each other in a gesture of empathy (St John's, midsummer). Harvest (gratitude for the abundance of nature) and Michaelmas (overcoming our dragons) lead towards Martinmas (the lantern festival, which recalls when St Martin shared his light, food and clothing with the poor), and Advent in the winter, looking inward at the little spark of light which glows at Christmas with the coming of Jesus, bringing love as a gift to the earth. Candlemas and the spring festivals lead once again to new life and rebirth. These are the most common festivals celebrated in a European Steiner kindergarten. Although seemingly religious, they are adapted to the seasons, to the group, and to nature, and in many cases, never mention any of the figures, but instead celebrate the intention and impulse connected with the festival.

Multicultural festivals could be an integral part of the kindergarten where a child is from another faith or culture. It is important to involve the parents and families by acknowledging, understanding and accepting their festivals (religious, seasonal and cultural), and then living into them so that they can become a reality for all concerned.

There are many similarities between festivals of different cultures, and often the themes overlap. Diwali, Martinmas, Channuka and Advent occur at the same time of the year, and bring light into the darkness.

In some kindergartens the cultural and religious celebrations are not celebrated overtly. Instead, they celebrate a seasonal festival which carries the same impulse: for instance, Easter, which is about rebirth, and reflects spring in nature; the egg hatching the chick; the caterpillar transforming into a butterfly; and the bulb growing a flower.

Development of a festival

As mentioned above, thought, care and careful preparation go into the development and implementation of a festival when undertaken with the children. Below I have written a description of one of the festivals which I developed for my own kindergarten.

Figure 7.2 Diwali

The festival of Diwali

One year, I had three children in the kindergarten who celebrated the festival of Diwali in some form at home, and as the parents and children often spoke about their experiences, I decided to celebrate it with all the children in the kindergarten. My first thought was how to begin to relate to this festival when I had little knowledge of the culture, history and so on, so I enlisted the help of the parents in developing my own understanding, and also undertook some research.

History

Diwali or Deepavali falls sometime between October and November on a moonless night. (Nature makes it the darkest night but mankind makes it the brightest!) Diwali means 'Row of Light' or 'Festival of Light' and is widely celebrated by Hindus throughout the world. (And by almost everyone, so I'm told, in India.) It contains age-old symbols: the triumph of light over darkness; and of good over evil. The story of Rama and Sita is told and the goddess Lakshmi is worshipped. Homes are cleaned and decorated, lamps and lights are acquired and food is prepared. There are celebrations with feasts, lights, dancing and fireworks.

Many of the above fit well into the kindergarten at this time of year as we prepare for Martinmas, Guy Fawkes and Advent. However, we found the story of Rama and Sita too complicated for our kindergarten children, so I wrote my own which was told leading up to and on the day of the festival.

The story

Once upon a time there lived a mother and father who had many children, and the youngest was called Anju. One day Anju woke to find that everyone was busy, cleaning and dusting, painting and scrubbing, sewing and cooking.

'Ma, what is happening?' he asked.

'Anju, tonight I will tell you,' said mother, and so she did.

63

That night when Anju was tucked up in bed. his mother told him the story of the festival of Diwali.

'Anju, we need to clean our house to be ready for a visit from Lakshmi, for she will bring us wealth and plenty, nice clothes, food to eat and happiness to our family. But she will only visit houses that are clean and tidy. Lazy people who never work and don't bother to clean and tidy their homes never have a visit from Lakshmi, and so are never happy and always grumble about how they live. If we are kind and cheerful, however, she will shower blessings over us.'

'How can she see how clean our house is, Ma?' asked Anju.

'At Diwali we light our houses with lamps filled with oil, or many candles, so that every corner is bright. That is why we make lots of little clay dishes to hold the candles or oil in. Tomorrow you will see. Goodnight, Anju,' said his mother.

The next day Anju woke early and the house was already filled with joyous sounds. He put on his new clothes and helped to draw the *rangoli* designs with coloured sand on the floor. When they had laid out the food and flowers everywhere, they put the oil lamps and candles onto every shelf and into every corner so that the house was filled with rows and rows of lights. In the evening Mother and Father lit them all and soon friends began to arrive, bringing gifts of sweet things for the family. Anju handed round food and more sweets to the visitors and they all made music together and danced and talked until quite late.

Anju was tired when everyone went outside, 'It's so dark, Ma,' he said.

'Not for long, Anju,' said his mother.

Suddenly the sky was filled with bangs and whizzes as fireworks lit up the dark sky, raining stars down on the children below. Anju and his brothers and sisters took sparklers to the children who had none, so that they could light up the darkness too, and those children's smiles lit up Anju's heart.

That night, when his mother tucked Anju up in bed he asked sleepily; 'Ma, did Lakshmi come to our house? I didn't see her.'

And his mother answered, 'Of course she did, Anju, for when happiness, light and love enter our hearts it is Lakshmi who puts them there. Didn't you feel them today?' But there was no reply, for Anju was fast asleep.

Preparation

In the kindergarten we made clay *Divas* – the lamps to hold nightlights – and cleaned the kindergarten, even the cobwebs in the corners! The nature table was covered with drapes of red and gold, and the parents supplied me with material and donated costumes and instruments.

The day of the festival

On the morning the children arrived to a very decorated room, red muslins and lots of gold and brass, the clothes laid out and flowers and lamps everywhere.

We set the table and prepared the food: buttered warm naan bread (different flavours) and cut-up *exotic* fruit. We then washed and dressed in our bright Indian clothes: muslins and scarves, saris, veils, cloaks and hats, all draped with care. Then we lit the festival candle, and danced together to the recorder and bells, holding and waving our brightly coloured sashes to Indian songs we had learned. Weaving in and out of a circle we made star patterns (joined by some of our parents who really knew what they were doing).

Then each child lit their light from the festival candle and carried it to the table, and soon it was lit with a long row of candles. We ate warmed naan bread and fruit and it was all delicious.

At story time, when the children returned from outside, they found the room in darkness, and in the centre of the story ring was a circle of their lit candles. In the middle of that was a big pot with sticks in it!

After the story we lit those sticks: sparklers! (indoor ones, of course). And when we came to blow out the candles to take home . . . oh, what a surprise: jellied fruits, and one for each child.

Lakshmi had visited our kindergarten this day.

The inclusion of this festival in my kindergarten made an enormous difference to the families and children. All the parents became involved, taking an interest, dressing up, preparing food, and started to look at their own cultural heritage.

Figure 7.3 Multicultural festival

The enthusiasm for multicultural festivals took on a new impulse, and we had many parents' evenings around the theme. The parents became more interested in each other, and out of this impulse, a larger festival developed which became fixed in the calendar: one at which all parents contributed and shared a little of their own culture with the other families, and with the children. For want of a better word, we called it our 'Summer Multicultural Festival'.

One year, in a group of eighteen children, we had over fourteen different cultures represented, each bringing a song or game, dressing-up clothes and food: the English brought strawberries, sandwiches and skipping ropes and hula hoops; the Germans brought stilts and Black Forest gateau; the Italians brought pizza and a wonderful game of flipping bottle tops; the Spanish acted out a bull fight song; the South Africans brought some musical instruments; the Irish brought a musician playing the harp; the Japanese some origami and brush painting, and some delicious sushi; the Chinese made lanterns with the children, and a puppet play; and so on . . . a treat for the children, teachers and parents.

Many kindergartens in the UK today have children from a wide variety of cultures who have integrated into the community. In some cases, where the cultures have not integrated, or there are new arrivals, celebrating multicultural festivals carries the impulse of inclusion, where all feel valued and acknowledged, and the wider community can learn from each other and be accepted into the culture of the kindergarten community. When the traditional English, Welsh, Scottish or Irish festivals are celebrated, the community can also become familiar with the country they have come to visit. This openness to each other is the impulse carried in the Whitsun festival, where songs are shared in different languages.

Storytelling and puppetry

Storytelling

Storytelling is and always has been a central activity of human life: it is one of the ways in which we learn about the world and make sense of our experiences. By giving children the experience of listening we enliven their imaginations and fantasy, and educate their memory. We help them to understand their world and to become effective communicators and listeners.

Family or stories from personal experience are the easiest way to begin, and children love nothing more than to hear about themselves.

It is easy to develop these stories and to add to them, thus bringing in some fantasy. It is a good way of bringing in an event which is about to happen (holiday, hospital), or to moralise a little (brush teeth, accident crossing the road), or to encourage positive behaviour (putting on the clothes that are laid out, being kind to friends, etc.).

Next is learning stories, so that they can be told rather than read to the children. The reason for this is that it enables the children to form their own pictures. There is nothing wrong with reading stories to the child either, but the effort of learning the story beforehand engages the will and allows you to add something of yourself to the story, which is felt inwardly by the child. Reading together and showing the child the pictures – we call it 'reading the pictures' – shows the children how to care for and handle books properly.

Animal stories (not fables which come at a later age) are always fun, for animals appeal to the feeling nature of the child; they can get up to mischief, be naughty and get away with it . . . something we 'moral' humans can't. Folk tales bring alive other cultures and broadens their world.

Fairy tales are told to older children and help their inner life to become flexible and active. They give wings to feeling, fire the will, stimulate thinking, and allow the children to experience emotions such as joy, sympathy, fear and courage. These work on their inner life, allowing them to develop a moral discernment of good and evil and an inner strength; courage to overcome and face the tasks and tests of life to come.

The stories we choose in the kindergarten are not moralising or cautionary tales, but bearers of underlying moral truths. These truths are not explained but are left to continue working in the child's imagination, their feeling and will. Dr Von Kugelgen, from the International Waldorf Kindergarten Association, quoted Steiner as saying; 'Fairy tales are healing to the soul of a child . . . The human soul has an inextinguishable need to have the substance of fairy tales flow through its veins, just as the body needs to have nourishing substances circulate through it' (Von Kugelgen 1993:47). The fairy tale engenders a dreamlike consciousness, which radiates feeling, and is filled with images.

The wisdom in fairy tales speaks figuratively of change, enchantment and solution – and with this, the secret of humanity. The child can sympathise with them right away, and all the 'cruelty' which we see in the dance around the wolf at the end of *Red Riding Hood* is for the child nothing other than the victory of good over bad.

> 'Fairy-tale children' experience more, they can express themselves more fully either in words or through art, are open, can listen better, and display greater pleasure in creative endeavours. They form thoughts into well-structured sentences containing a more extensive vocabulary.
>
> (Von Kugelgen 1993:48)

When telling fairy tales, it is important not to arouse fear by using drama in the voice. They are told with a gentle dreamy lilting 'storytelling voice'.

There are certain fairy tales suitable for different ages. The teacher needs to choose stories which work with the children and which suit their age or individual characteristics. Sometimes stories are also chosen carefully to deal with a particular situation, or for therapy purposes. The most important consideration is the storyteller's own relationship to the story. The teacher needs to understand it and be comfortable with it.

Puppetry

For centuries now, puppet plays have been a source of pleasure. It does not matter whether the text is in one language or another, whether the story is presented in a shopping centre or in a palace, or whether the puppets are worked by strings, worn on the hands, moved by rods or whatever. Puppets are always fascinating to human beings. These miniature actors are surrounded by an atmosphere of reality and fantasy, of magic, mystery and dreams and, in addition, the humour and satire afford delightful entertainment.

In these little figures there is a mysterious power, which can cast such a spell over children and grown-ups alike that they are bewitched into

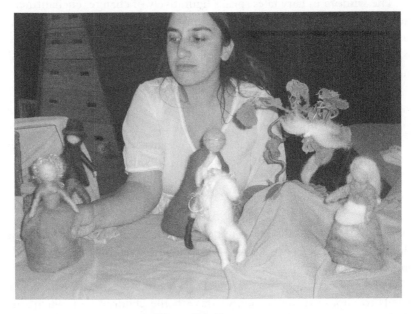

Figure 8.1 Puppetry

imagining living creatures of flesh and blood in place of puppets made of wood or other materials. The audience sees only what they want to see; indeed, they are so gripped by the play that the imagination makes its own contribution and they see much more: laughing and weeping, and the whole gamut of emotions mirrored in the puppet faces.

In recent years there has been a gratifying increase in the number of amateur puppet groups. These groups are a living source of creative and artistic talent and their number is growing from day to day. One finds puppet groups in children's hospitals, in the treatment of disturbances, special needs, traffic education, war-torn countries, AIDS education, therapy for speech defects and much more. Where a child can manipulate a puppet they take on a different role. The puppet can talk and act as the child wishes and 'it's all safe'. When a child talks *to* a puppet, the puppet actually acts as a mediator, as a third person. The child therefore does not feel confronted by another ego, but feels that they are free to speak or react safely, and will not be judged.

In an article on the art of the Marionette theatre, Von Kugelgen (1993), quoted Steiner as saying, 'Puppetry is a remedy against the ravages of civilisation'.

Steiner always responded to questions which were asked of him In 1917, Leonhard Gem and Hedwig Hauck (painters and sculptors) asked Steiner for advice on how to build a puppet theatre for a day-care centre (the children were four to twelve years old). Steiner became deeply involved in this, and insisted that the marionettes should hang on threads tied directly to the fingers (not a cross bar), directed from above, that only marionettes were appropriate for the presentation of fairy tales and that a narrator should read the story from outside the curtain.

Steiner was particularly interested in stage lighting and scenery, and everything was done with one purpose in mind. He said, 'we must do everything in our power to help the children to develop fantasy!' (Von Kugelgen, 1993:47).

Puppet shows nourish the feeling life and the senses. They contain speech and music, colour and movement: a full artistic experience. The movement of the puppets should be peaceful (not be jerky like cartoons, or fast like Punch and Judy). The children take these movements into their beings, and it affects their own sense of movement. Puppetry also helps develop the memory and increases vocabulary and communication skills.

In the kindergarten many different forms of puppetry are used: finger and hand puppets; tabletop puppet shows; and full fairy tales performed with marionettes.

In play little figures are used to make up scenes on the floor and they interact with each other. This is particularly suitable for the younger children.

However presented, the puppet shows are a full artistic experience. The scene is made (sometimes with the children) and then covered with a cloth. The 'unveiling' when it begins – usually to music played simply on a lyre (children's harp) or kalimba (a kind of thumb piano) – draws the children into the puppet show. It has a beginning, middle and end, which is complete and satisfying for them, containing language, movement, music and colour, but the teacher or adult is responsible for what happens, which gives the children a feeling of security. The children can see how adults deal with mistakes, which reassures them that things are

Figure 8.2 A child's puppet show

not always perfect. Everything is visible to them. They get a picture of the whole, and the past, present and future is before them.

Very often larger puppet shows are presented after the story has been told for a few days before. The repetition of the story helps the memory and enables the children to build their own pictures before they are presented with visual ones. Because of the repetition they can recreate the stories in play or their own puppet shows. They generally do not use the teachers' puppets but adapt or make their own.

The puppet pocket apron (worn by the adult) has decorated pockets in which the finger or standing puppets 'live'. They come out to tell stories or sing rhymes, or a familiar story can also be told using the puppets from different pockets to tell the story. There are farm aprons, tree aprons, house aprons and so on. Silk cloths are used to cover the lap on which to act out the story. The apron is particularly suitable for younger children and toddlers, who enjoy the magical appearance and disappearance of the puppets.

Puppetry is not only enriching for the children but also for the puppeteers, for there is no end to the creativity.

9 | Working within the Early Years Foundation Stage (EYFS)

Since the introduction of the voucher scheme with its Desirable Learning Outcomes, and then the Foundation Stage Curriculum, the majority of Steiner Waldorf kindergartens registered for the early years funding for three and four year olds. When, in 2008, the Early Years Foundation Stage (EYFS) was introduced, all Steiner kindergartens had to comply with the requirements for all settings that take children from birth to five, and with the independent school regulations for five to six year olds.

Exemptions

However the statutory nature of the Early Years Foundation Stage has highlighted some issues which resulted in an exemptions process being introduced, so that the specific educational approach and philosophical differences could be taken into account. It has been recognised that the particular issues, which could not be met by Steiner Early Childhood Education, are the formal introduction of letters (reading and writing under the Communication, Language and Literacy section of the Learning and Development Requirements) and the inclusion of ICT and electronic gadgetry (we have what we call 'warm' technology, such as woodwork tools, spinning wheels, cookers, juicers, etc.). Although the exemptions process was bureaucratic and time-consuming, it was reviewed in 2012, when the new EYFS was introduced. Since then new exemptions have been applied for under the umbrella organisation the Steiner Waldorf Schools Fellowship. These exemptions are applied for by all members, whether they are schools, academies, independent kindergartens, day care or childminders. The inspectors who visit ask to see the above, and the settings are not judged against the exempt areas, or against those which have been modified. The exemptions are granted in full for the whole of the literacy programme, which includes the two goals of reading and writing. The majority of settings are also exempt from the completion and submission of the EYFS profile. The Steiner profile is completed instead, which refers to the EYFS prime areas of learning in some cases, and to the Early Learning Goals (ELG).

In general, the new EYFS 2014 is much less prescriptive, and pays less heed to the areas which we could see as fitting in with the Steiner Waldorf approach, such as the themes and principles: the Unique Child, Positive Relationships and Enabling Environments. In 2010, we published a 'read-over' document – called the 'Guide to the Early Years Foundation Stage in Steiner Settings' – which highlighted how we met, or could work with these, and we commented on each of the commitments underpinning the principles, as well as on other parts of the EYFS as it stood at that time. Although this is still available online, we have introduced a new 'read over' document to which I will refer below when highlighting some of the similarities or differences between the EYFS and Steiner practice.

EYFS principles

EYFS overarching principle: a unique child

> Every child is a unique child, who is constantly learning and can be resilient, capable, confident and self-assured.
>
> (EYFS 2014:6)

The Steiner concept is that everything that surrounds young children, both visible and invisible, has an impact on them. An understanding of human development underpins all Steiner practice. It takes account of the whole child, including the spiritual and soul qualities, and believes that children's development and learning flourishes in a calm, peaceful, predictable, familiar and unhurried environment, which recognises the child's sensory sensitivities, all of which help the child develop resilience. The different activities, with their diverse but nurturing qualities, contribute to the gradual unfolding of the child's gifts, allowing them to become well-balanced in physical, emotional and cognitive development. Practitioners allow children time to develop these capacities at their own pace within a well-structured and child-friendly environment. Many items are made as gifts for family members and the home, and the graces of gratitude and thankfulness are practised through action and deed.

EYFS principle: positive relationships

> Children learn to be strong and independent through positive relationships.
>
> (EYFS 2014:6)

The development of social skills and awareness of others are preconditions to formal learning, and prepare children for the behaviour that is required once children are in the classroom situation. Imitation is one of the most effective and natural means of learning at this age, and practitioners perform their tasks consciously and carefully, aware that they may be models worthy of imitation.

The mixed-age family-style groupings help with social relationships, and the children are encouraged to share, work together, care for each other and respect the needs of others. The behaviour of children is moulded by what surrounds them. Kindness is practised by practitioners and encouraged in the children, and they learn to trust the adults around them. Traditional fairy tales and nature stories address the feeling realm and gradually awaken a fine moral sense for knowing right from wrong. The practitioner practises tolerance and patience, and in cases of challenging behaviour, addresses the behaviour, not the child.

The practitioner (key worker) and other helpers work as a team, providing a family environment away from home. Strong connections are

Figure 9.1 Building relationships

made and maintained with the child's family/carers, and a bridge is built between home and school.

EYFS principle: enabling environments

Children learn and develop well in enabling environments, in which their experiences respond to their individual needs and there is a strong partnership between practitioners and parents and/or carers.

(EYFS 2014:6)

The children are encouraged to appreciate the natural world in order to help them value its gifts, and to understand its processes and the patterns of the seasons. The beauty of nature, plants, insects and animals is brought to the children with awe and wonder. The use of natural materials in play and craft fosters a connection with the natural world; that is, the foundations of a respect for the environment and all it provides. Domestic tasks provide opportunities for elementary experiences of science and the four elements. When children make toys from sheep's wool, wood, felt, cotton and other natural materials they learn about the origin of these materials. Domestic activity needs proper tools, therefore knives, peelers, saws, hand drills and proper gardening tools are provided so that they can learn to use these tools in a safe and appropriate manner.

Figure 9.2 Spring cleaning

Children are encouraged to look after the kindergarten equipment, sanding and oiling wooden furniture and toys, mending things that break, washing clothes and doing other simple tasks, which children and adults can do together. Through organic gardening, recycling and taking care of our immediate environment we create a basis to care for our world, others and ourselves.

EYFS principle: Learning and development

Children develop and learn in different ways and at different rates. The framework covers the education and care of all children in early years provision including children with special educational needs and disabilities.

(EYFS 2014:6)

It is part of the Steiner curriculum that physical, emotional, social, spiritual and cognitive development work and develop equally in each child; these are all equally important and interconnected. Young children need to experience the relevance of their world before they separate themselves from it, and begin to analyse it in a detached way. Learning gains meaning by its relevance to life and should not be separated from the business of daily living.

Cognitive, social, emotional and physical skills are accorded equal value and many different competencies are developed. Activities reflect the concerns, interests and developmental stages of the child, and the carefully structured environment is designed to foster both personal and social learning. Both the intellectual and physical development of the child are allowed to unfold at their own pace and time, and everything provided within the setting underpins more formal learning which takes place at a later stage.

Teaching is by example rather than by direct instruction, and is integrated rather than subject-based. The framework is adapted to the child. In recognition of its vital role in early education, and central to the kindergarten experience, children are encouraged to find their own learning situations in child-initiated free and creative play, in which they

Figure 9.3 Life skills

develop, in particular, positive social skills and empathy towards each other. The practitioners aid and facilitate the development of life skills over time that then become good habits, supporting the child's learning. Children then become motivated and independent learners.

Learning and development requirements

In the new EYFS, the areas of learning and development are broken down into:

- seven areas of learning and development;
- early learning goals;
- assessment requirements.

There is little difficulty in meeting some, and working towards all the above, with obvious exceptions in areas where there are fundamental curriculum differences. We have exemptions or modifications for those, such as the literacy programme with reading and writing, or mathematics with its written number, and of course, the requirement to have electronic gadgetry. Below is highlighted how these exemptions are attained with little difficulty, and in many cases, with good or outstanding results in Ofsted Inspection reports.

I have included some examples of how certain areas of the Learning and Development requirements are met in Steiner kindergartens. The charts are taken from the read-over document (see Tables 9.1 and 9.2).

Personal, social and emotional development

These areas are particularly strong in Steiner practice, both in social development and for the dispositions and attitudes of the children. As you can see in the previous chapters, the children, when working out of imitation and supported by the staff and their peers, are able to become independent learners, who form good relationships with adults and peers and thus an integrated and harmonious group. The children have a highly developed moral sense and are sensitive to the needs and feelings of others. It is wonderful to see the older children in the mixed-age kindergartens helping the younger to dress, with play and developing a general caring attitude.

Communication and language and physical development

Children develop competence in talking, listening and in the ability to use words as they speak freely and learn to listen to others. Good speech and the development of aural skills are promoted. Concentration is on the oral tradition and the children listen to many wonderful stories, which belong to the literary heritage of the culture of childhood. A well-told story creates an appreciation for the human voice, and the beauty and rhythms of language. It also helps to extend vocabulary and to aid the development of a good memory. Through storytelling and story-hearing, the children partake in the structuring processes of narrative, in which complex information is put into meaningful context. Children leave kindergarten with a rich and varied repertoire of songs, stories and poems. This might also include verses in French or German or other languages (see Chapter 12). These stages of pre-literacy are an important preparation for the formal introduction of reading and writing, which requires clear listening and speaking, good memory, an intuitive sense for language structure, an enjoyment of language, as well manual skills and hand-eye coordination.

Children engage in many activities, such as sewing and weaving, which develop hand-eye coordination, manual dexterity and orientation (a useful preparation for reading print from left to right). Children also discuss their own drawings and take great delight in telling stories by 'reading' their pictures. This activity promotes the development of verbal skills and frees the narrative from the printed text, thus encouraging children to use their own words. Many children also set out or perform puppet shows and develop dramatic skills through working

Figure 9.4 Weaving

with narrative and dialogue. Painting and drawing help with balance and symmetry, and most five year olds are able to write their own name. Children experience the musicality of language and its social aspects through playing ring games and doing Eurythmy (see Chapter 12); a form of movement which works with language and music.

The combination of these activities cultivates a love of language, promotes fluency and allows the children time to become really familiar with the spoken word: the best preparation and foundation for the subsequent development of literacy. Use of language also affects cognitive development, as well as chosen words and good syntax support clear thinking.

Problem-solving, reasoning and numeracy

Mathematics and the use of mathematical language are integrated into the daily rhythm. This might take place at the table where food is prepared (sliced carrots make wonderful natural circles and have the added virtue of being able to be eaten later in soup!), and addition and subtraction (or more or less), weight, measure, quantity and shape are grasped in a practical manner, as part of daily life in cooking and baking. Mealtimes offer an opportunity for the moral, social and mathematical to work together as children engage in place–setting and the sharing of food, which has been prepared earlier for everyone to eat.

Through movement games, children recognise and recreate patterns: in, out, alternate, in front of, behind. Natural objects such as acorns, pine cones, conkers and shells are sorted, ordered and counted, as part of spontaneous play. Children are directly involved in mathematical experience and use mathematical language in a natural way, which is usually embedded in a social and moral context. Learning experiences for the young child are not separated from the business of daily living: learning gains meaning by its relevance to life.

Children develop a good relationship with the natural world. They learn to value its gifts and to understand its processes and patterns of change. Domestic tasks provide opportunities for elementary experiences in science and good use is made of the four elements. Family participation is encouraged and teachers, working with parents, create

Figure 9.5 Building and tying

'birthday stories' based on the child's personal biography, which are told at special ceremonies to which families are invited. Festivals and community events enable children to begin to know about their own and others' culture and beliefs. Awe and wonder in the natural world is enhanced through the lack of direct instruction and the use of fantasy and imagination by the adults.

People in the community who practise a particular craft, or who have special skills, are often invited to visit the kindergarten, and many teachers take their children for short local walks and visits. An interest in the natural world, the use of tools and 'warm' technology help the children to find out and explore how their world works.

Technology

Children are not exposed to any form of programmable toy or electronic technology such as TV or computers, and parents are discouraged from

Figure 9.6 Warm technology

providing them at home. We have 'warm technology', such as a hand-driven grain mill, an apple juice press, scales, a spinning wheel and various woodwork tools. 'Warm technology' gives the child a true picture of the function of a machine as an extension of their body. It also supports the child's thinking and physical skills in an age-appropriate way, since thinking in a young child is expressed mainly in a physical way. Exemptions have been granted in this area.

Physical development

The children have constant opportunities to build up their small and large motor skills, through domestic and creative activities, and to practise and enjoy the physical environment, both indoors and out.

Creative development

Children have access to a variety of materials which are used for imaginative play, crafts, dance, puppetry and drama. These express and communicate their ideas and fulfil all the requirements.

Questions that arise

There are a number of areas where questions about the pedagogical approach arise, specifically: the use of questioning to enhance and broaden the child's learning; and the lack of display of the children's work.

Questioning children

Children learn as a result of exploration and discovery, as well as through imitation of adults and the world around them. The Steiner philosophy considers that children do not need adults to question what and why they do things, only to support and encourage, and that can be done without words! The environment is already noisy, busy, stimulating. Children tend to switch off from these constant stimulations, build a shell around themselves, stop listening, become overstimulated, constantly expect praise and support. Is this what is wanted? No. Quiet supportive confirmation of their explorations into life is all that is required. Children just need space, time and the right environment to develop at their own pace.

Why children's work is not displayed

Looking at the pieces of work that children produce one can see not only their skills and developing capacities, but also indications of individual strengths and weaknesses, both currently and in the future. In children's drawings particularly, one can see significant indicators of developmental stages. For these reasons careful note is taken of everything that the children produce, which includes paying attention to what the children may want to tell us about their work. It is also part of the reverence and respect that are shown to everyone that children's efforts are appreciated and taken care of, thus setting a good example.

For young children, however, the process is much more important than the result, and viewing the display is less satisfactory than its production. Children often ignore their paintings once they are complete and they have shown them to an adult. Displays of work also invite comparison and judgements and we believe these should be avoided in children under seven.

Figure 9.7 Joint drawing activity

Instead, after the teacher has appreciated and taken note both of the child at work and of the product of the work, this will either be carefully put aside, ready for the child to take home (pictures may be rolled and tied with wool, other projects wrapped), or the teacher may keep the piece of work to give to the family at the end of term, at the end of the school year, or at the next festival if the project is directly related to the festival. For example, pom-pom chicks may be gathered in a nest of straw as they are completed, ready to give out at the spring festival, or the whole year's spread of paintings (one from each week) will be collected in a folder that the child has made, and given to the parents at the end of the school year.

Saving the drawings and paintings in this way enables the teacher to gain an overview of the child's progress, which will be discussed at an individual meeting with the parents. Alternatively, the child may take their drawings home more frequently, but the teacher will keep those that are particularly developmentally significant in the child's file, as part of a portfolio.

In this way children are shown that their work is valuable and to be taken care of, and that the work of producing it is worthwhile and noted, but they are not encouraged to dwell upon it after it is complete.

Table 9.1 Examples from the 'read-over' document

EYFS AREAS OF LEARNING	ELG	STEINER WALDORF ASPECTS OF LEARNING
PRIME AREAS	These develop in response to relationships and experiences, and run through and support learning in other areas (Development Matters pg.4).	
Communication and language Involves giving children opportunities to speak and listen in a range of situations and to develop their confidence and skills in expressing themselves.	**01: Listening and attention** Children listen attentively in a range of situations. They listen to stories, accurately anticipating key events, and respond to what they hear with relevant comments, questions or actions. They give their attention to what others say and respond appropriately, while engaged in another activity. **02: Understanding** Children follow instructions involving several ideas or actions. *They demonstrate understanding in response to stories or events or when recounting their experiences.*	**01: Stories, songs and rhymes: hear with rich vocabulary, repeatedly, delivered by human voice, with beautiful rhythm and/or foreign language:** * developing an aural memory; listen attentively and enjoy a traditional fairy, folk nature tale-told true to cultural heritage and told in exactly the same way many consecutive times; listen and watch attentively to a puppet show; may be chosen to help with the puppet show once it has been repeated a few times – therefore anticipating the next part; listen to each other; listen attentively to the practitioner's comments and respond appropriately. **02: Group activities – play, domestic or creative work, meal times:** * listen attentively to the practitioner's comments and respond appropriately; through conversations or actions interact appropriately with peers.

(continued)

Table 9.1 (continued)

EYFS AREAS OF LEARNING	ELG	STEINER WALDORF ASPECTS OF LEARNING
		Develop a Listening Disposition: *ability to listen to (age-appropriate) needs and feelings of self and of others; *ability to respond to (age-appropriate) needs and feelings of self and of others; ability to be interactive, compromise, be flexible.
	03: Speaking Children express themselves effectively, showing awareness of listeners' needs. They use part, present and future forms accurately when talking about events that have happened or are to happen in the future. They develop their own narratives and explanations by connecting ideas or events.	03: They develop their own narratives and explanations by connecting ideas or events. *speak freely (and listen) to each other during activities; through conversations and or actions: interact appropriately with peers; talk about observations of any activity or environment, etc.; imitate the polite manner of speaking modelled by the adults in the setting; have opportunities throughout each session to express needs and feelings. Puppet show or acting: *recreate songs, rhymes and stories; use a combination of a known story and inventing new parts; imagination to make up own song, rhyme or story. Creative Play: *dress up and pretend, perhaps stimulated by heard stories or personal experiences; create own imaginative world; home, work, adventure – using simple improvised, beautiful and natural props from environment; create a story with a story line; imitate language in own self-initiated and imaginative play; talk about play with peers or adults – story line, perceptions, ideas, feelings.

*interact, negotiate and cooperate with peers in free creative play – communicating the story line, perceptions, ideas and or feelings; use emergent writing in own style creating props for creative play; e.g. tickets for a train or show, etc.; use emergent writing and mark making in own style; read pretend writing; use crayons for drawing or emergent writing; imitate the writing of their own name; read own name and names of friends; read pictures in a story book, creating a story with sequence.

Ring time – traditional games, songs and rhymes given in clear adult speech,rhythmically and routinely performed or sung beautifully:

*rhymes, riddles and games: extend vocabulary with word play e.g. 'horsey-borsey'; enjoy, participate and imitate gestures and words, rhymes and sounds of poems, or songs; take part in rhymes, songs, games and poems shared in different languages; games: Participate; e.g. 'I spy', or similar game, fostering phonological awareness of beginning and end syllables in words. Connecting words and meanings through engagement with and repetition of words and movements.

Group activities – play, domestic or creative work, meal and snack times:

*share ideas and experiences; take part in counting games, rhymes, riddles, etc.

Domestic work:

*imitation of names of tools and actions; talk about domestic activities.

Table 9.2 EYFS areas of learning

EYFS AREAS OF LEARNING	ELG	STEINER WALDORF ASPECTS OF LEARNING
PRIME AREAS	These develop in response to relationships and experiences, and run through and support learning in other areas (Development Matters pg.4).	
Mathematics	11 Numbers – MODIFIED: Children *orally count reliably with numbers from 1 to 20, place them in order and say which number is one more or one less than a given number. Using quantities and objects in everyday activities and play, they add and subtract two single-digit numbers and count on or back to find the answer. In everyday activities and play they solve problems, including doubling, halving and sharing.*	11: Practice in counting in sequence: * number rhymes, finger rhymes, nursery rhymes and songs; observing the older children count when setting the table, etc.; discussions among children who can count, and counting on or counting back, up or down; taking turns or sharing toys, etc. Practice in counting and solving practical problems, using the 'quality' of numbers and measures: * in each child's birthday celebration, events in the child's past are highlighted, using specific 'milestones' to represent each passing year; setting the table – number of children present, chairs, bowls, crockery and cutlery; cooking; quantities and measuring; craft; drawing, painting, sewing, woodwork, gardening; play; building with blocks and more challenging natural shapes; doll corner; sandpit; tidying; discussions among children: comparison of ages of people and exchanging simple sums; may write numerals as emergent writing.

12 Shape, space and measures: Children use everyday language to talk about size, weight, capacity, position, distance, time and money to compare quantities and objects and to solve problems. They recognise, create and describe patterns. They explore characteristics of everyday objects and shapes and use mathematical language to describe them.

12: Creating patterns, ordering; block play; craft and art work; tidying.

Everyday (mathematical) language that is developed through the exploration, observation, reflection, and discovery of different qualities of shape, space and measures:

- giving and taking, losing and gaining, sharing, more than, bigger than, less than, smaller than, fewer, greater (precursor to using the 4 operations)
- circle, oblong, square, triangle, etc. (names of shapes)
- taller, longer, shorter, thinner, fatter, wider, broader, heavy-weight, light-weight, full, half-full, empty (comparisons and differences between shapes and spaces)
- late, early, yesterday, last year, today, tomorrow, next month, days of the week (language around time)
- language around space: near, far away, close to, behind, in front of, through.

(continued)

Table 9.2 (continued)

EYFS AREAS OF LEARNING	ELG	STEINER WALDORF ASPECTS OF LEARNING
		* provision of a rich interesting environment with an emphasis on beautiful, descriptive and accurate language; plenty of beautiful singing and music (human voice and real instruments) giving a real experience of time measured in rhythm and melody; receptive rather than active approach of practitioner enabling the child to relax and observe and reflect, and to speak and to be heard; gentle, slow and relaxed pace of transitions and routines that allow for plenty of opportunity among the children to discuss their own observations and comparisons of numbers, size, shape, space and measures; singing, dancing, poetry, stories, puppet shows; Eurythmy; games
		* domestic work – working in sequence, ordering, tidying, chopping carrot circles, sewing a triangle shape
		* creative work – woodwork, craft, painting, drawing
		* creative play – climbing frame, sandpit, doll corner, house building, blocks creating a small world, role play, own shows
		* following the daily, weekly, seasonal and festival routines, rhythms and celebrations
		* coherent tidy routines – long sticks in long basket, round logs in round basket, cloths folded into squares, ropes wound into spirals, etc.

10 | Observation, assessment and planning

It is a requirement to undertake observation and assessment as part of the Early Years Foundation Stage (EYFS), and work within the guidance and guidelines provided in this area, including the submission of the EYFS Profile (for five year olds) to the Local Authority. Steiner Waldorf kindergartens in the main have exemptions from the whole section on assessment at the end of the EYFS, including the completion and submission of the profile (see Appendix 1: Exemptions and modifications to EYFS). However, observation and assessment is done, in fact, extremely thoroughly, within the Steiner kindergarten, as described below

The Steiner Waldorf approach to observation and assessment

Observation is the basis for formative assessment and plays an important part in the practitioner's work. Detailed observation is necessary to gain an understanding of each child's holistic development and educational progress. The emphasis is on observing the whole child, both in the kindergarten and family. This is an ongoing process of picture-building, and it begins with the first meeting of teacher, parent and child at the initial interview, and concludes at the end of the child's time in kindergarten. Parents generally contribute to the overall picture in the assessment process, and any observations are regularly shared with the parents.

Observations can be expressed in a variety of forms; for instance, notes, photographs, child records, child study, Individual Education

Plan (IEP), profile and end-of-year report, or a specially designated meeting with the parents.

Research undertaken in Steiner kindergartens has been written up in a book, which gives a good description of this (see *Meeting the Child in Steiner Kindergartens: An Exploration of Beliefs, Values and Practices* (Parker-Rees, 2011)).

Principles governing the process of picture-building

The kindergarten teacher:

- Observes the whole child: physical, emotional, social, cognitive and speech development;
- Understands that learning and development is, of course, a continuous process, and may wait patiently to watch these unfold;
- Uses insight rather than measurement. The question is 'Who are you?' rather than 'What can you do?'
- Makes an attempt to understand the unfolding character and destiny of the child;
- Makes developmentally appropriate observation; i.e. the importance of not fixing a child's development in time;
- Observes in different contexts within the rhythm of the day; e.g. play, snack time;
- Interprets observations; e.g. a stage of drawing, according to the guidelines given by Michaela Strauss in *Understanding Children's Drawings* (2007);
- Respects and refrains from hurrying the child's natural speed of development;
- Shares observations and insights with parents and practitioners;
- Meditates on the child, holds the child in their thoughts (a process termed as 'inner work');
- Works to develop an intuitive understanding of the child (to understand better one's observation and its significance);
- Is aware of and engaged in their own self-development.

Various processes of picture-building

Initial meeting with parents

In the initial meeting with parents and child, the kindergarten teacher observes the child's physicality, speech, social interaction and possibly activities such as drawing and some play. The interview with the parents provides information on the culture of the family, the home environment and routines, the child's health, preferences, possible difficulties or special needs. The interview serves the parents equally, by initiating them into the kindergarten ways and the wider expectations that the kindergarten may have for them. It establishes the beginnings of a long and very important cooperative partnership in the education of the child.

Ongoing observations and sharing with parents

The relationship between teacher and parent is deepened over time through a variety of means: an example may be a home visit, which is made at least once but sometimes several times in a year. Parents are provided with frequent opportunities to speak about their child, either informally at pick-up time, via the telephone, or in a more formal pre-arranged meeting. They are also invited to termly parent evenings, which offer them a chance to discuss the curriculum and ask any questions they might have.

Practitioners gain much-valued insights into the nature of the child through this well-fostered relationship. Equally, it allows the parents to share in and positively influence the evaluation of their child's progress and development.

Review and evaluation

Teachers and colleagues (assistants) evaluate on a daily or weekly basis about their planned, as well as ad-hoc child observations and notes, in order to review their work. Judgements made are likely to inform further planning, either for the whole group, part of the group or individual children: e.g. the oldest group may need extra time to finish their sewing; a child with a hearing problem needs to sit opposite the practitioner at snack time in order to lip-read better; another needs more attention than usual from the practitioner because his mother is in hospital, and so on.

Notes are made of children's achievements and milestones: for example, the quality of a finished project; who joined in singing at ring time for the first time; or who bravely climbed a small tree.

Child study

This is used to understand in detail a child's particular, individual needs. There are different formats for this. An example is that over the course of at least a week all the adults in contact with the child make detailed observations. These include a physical description (even of the way the child walks), personal mannerisms, social interaction, speech, play, etc. The teacher makes extensive written notes and then often shares these with the parents of the child, who are asked to contribute to the picture as well. Finally, the observations are shared in a meeting with other colleagues. A special verse for the child is chosen and then all carry the picture produced by the study in their thoughts and through sleep. A week later comments are exchanged and discussed further. This process frequently produces valuable insights which help to understand the child more deeply and often leads to changes in the relationship between adult and child, resulting in improvements to any problem. Even a small, almost undetectable change can have a powerful and positive effect on the child.

Individual education planning for children with additional needs

Although children's needs are normally met within group strategies, it can happen that a child has individual requirements and learning differences that call for expert advice and specific therapeutic measures. In this case, the practitioner draws up a plan supervised by a Special Educational Needs Coordinator (SENCO), often in connection with a child study. This document specifically states the child's needs and how the practitioner/setting attempts to meet them. Strategies and resources are listed and parents are asked to contribute and implement the remedies identified. Where possible the school doctor or eurythmist is also consulted and suggested therapy is followed.

Child records and reports

Keeping records is a statutory requirement and the initial interview, home visit reports, logs of meetings with parents, study and observation records, the profile, as well as evidence of children's work, are kept together in a file. This includes photographs of the child's work, and the child in situations where they are happy and playing, or working with others (and not performing for the camera). Also included are other reports and medical details, observation and action sheets, any individual plans and school-readiness checks, child study notes, etc. This document can be passed on to the child's school teacher, or go with the child when they leave the kindergarten.

At the end of each school year a written report is usually provided for the parents. Sometimes this summarises their child's development across the six areas of learning, in line with statutory requirements. Most importantly, it will also contain a short personal section for the child, a poem, photograph, drawing or picture.

Class one readiness assessment

Six-year-old children, who are at the end of the kindergarten period, may enter into the main school class one, which demands certain skills and readiness for formal learning. In order to ascertain the readiness of a child, kindergarten teachers, often together with others, assess maturity of movement, speech, drawing skills, social and emotional development, as well as physical health and development. Observations are recorded in a specially formatted profile or report, which is passed onto the class one teacher.

Figure 10.1 Patterns

If there is any doubt about the child's readiness or should they fall outside the cut-off dates for admission to the school, the school doctor or a member of the school admissions team observes the child and gives their recommendation. Parents are also consulted and a collaborative decision is reached. In cases of learning difficulties, learning support is sought and recommendations are given to the class teacher. As always, parents are involved in the process of planning for the special needs of their child.

Planning and preparation

The kindergarten teachers work together with colleagues to plan their work and prepare stories, songs, verses and activities appropriate to the children's age, the time of year (season/festival), or sometimes to an individual child's life situation.

Most kindergartens follow both long-term and weekly plans, though some practitioners may use their own individual planning formats. Planning is seen as a tool of organisation, as well as a form of communication with other colleagues and parents. Although all planning is necessarily structured within a certain format, it is used flexibly, and practitioners may divert from it if the need arises, such as when a visitor comes to present a special activity, or a sudden change of weather might provide an opportunity for a picnic in the garden.

Festivals, birthdays, parents' evenings, events, outings and the main seasonal activities (e.g. apple juicing) are outlined in the yearly plan. Although many activities – for example, ring time or snack time – occur daily and are purposely repetitive, they are normally still marked on daily plan, and are finely differentiated according to individual groups' or children's needs. Artistic activities, such as painting or domestic activities like baking, are pre-planned and take place on the same day each week, sometimes to meet the specific needs of certain groups of children. There are also activities that take place over a period of time according to the season, such as making lanterns in the autumn, or making spring baskets.

Individual's children's needs, though noted in the evaluation process, are met as far as possible through regular group activities. In the case of specific learning differences an IEP is used to help focus strategies and resources.

Preparation and review

Establishing a calm and nurturing environment that supports and encourages creativity in the child is an important part of the Steiner practitioner's preparation, and a considerable amount of time each day is spent preparing the room, activities and materials for the session, and reviewing them at the end of the day and week. Planning, preparation and review takes place with colleagues where possible, so that there is a seamless transition between sessions, aftercare, home and big school.

Inner and outer preparation

Where possible the staff meet in the morning to say a verse and prepare inwardly for the day ahead. They greet each other and share a moment of silence together before the busy day begins.

The kindergarten teacher also prepares inwardly for the group. Usually a picture is formed of each individual child and taken into sleep, or a verse said for a particular situation or child in need. Often this results in improved behaviour, or a story or activity which could help a particular situation comes to mind: and very often, as in a child study, a particularly difficult issue is resolved: a miracle!

Supervision

The EYFS 3.21 requires that providers put in place arrangements for the supervision of all staff. It says: 'Supervision should foster a culture of mutual support, teamwork and continuous improvement'. It also requires that time is given to discuss developmental issues, well-being and improve personal effectiveness.

In Steiner Waldorf settings, leadership is non-hierarchical. Therefore, this supervisory role may be taken on a rotational basis, and practitioners have developed ways of self-reflection, review and looking at appropriate training and helping colleagues settle into the life of the setting.

All staff meet on a weekly basis to study together and deepen their knowledge about the education, do their child study if planned, as well as administration or planning. They may also do a craft together, plan their ring time, sing or do an activity which meets and enhances social and emotional interaction, building empathy, friendships and improving communication. If they are an integral part of an all through Steiner school they also take part in weekly faculty meetings or college of teachers meetings, as the kindergarten is seen as the foundation of the school. Early years staff also meet together with those running parent and child groups, local childminders, and with local cluster groups, so that they can share good practice and form a holistic team in order to support the children and their families in a seamless way.

 # Working with parents and the first three years

Steiner Waldorf teachers are committed to establishing good relationships with parents and building the bridge between home and school, as the importance of a happy, smooth transition from home to school is recognised. The majority of kindergartens hold baby groups and/or parent and child sessions (birth to three years) and have a good rapport with the family

Figure 11.1 Craft group

before the child enters kindergarten. Teachers promote and emphasise the importance of close partnerships with parents and provide a focus for parent support. Links are also created with parents through a range of social and school-based events and activities, such as providing parenting or other workshops, craft sessions and celebrating festivals together.

Close liaison between parent and teacher is encouraged and the process of integration into the kindergarten is a gradual one.

The teacher informs themselves about the child, by meeting with the parents before the child joins the group, and filling out the child profile mentioned before. The child may have a slow integration into the group, with the parent visiting with the child if necessary. The teacher and assistant usually do a home visit during the first term, which is an opportunity to develop a closer relationship with the child. Regular parent evenings, with a themed talk and activity, provide an opportunity for parents to meet on a social basis, as well as familiarising the parents with the curriculum. The parents join the children for some festivals and puppet shows, and help is expected with the upkeep of the kindergarten, such as doing the washing, flower rota, providing organic fruit, joining the group for outings or assisting with an activity, such as helping with the woodwork or spinning.

Parent and child and baby groups

Most kindergartens begin with a baby group or parent and child group, which is where the children and parents are introduced to the ethos of the pedagogy. They usually form the basis of the kindergarten and school, and through them come the children into kindergarten, and then to school. They are usually situated in a hall close to the school, or where possible, take place in the same building. There are also many forest or woodland parent and child groups, where they meet outdoors for the entire session.

These provide a peaceful environment within which parent and child (toddler to around three) can play and talk with each other and to those around them. Since new parents are often insecure about their parenting skills, space is offered where parents can find the stillness in which to realise that they are already doing a great job. The trained leaders offer information and the parents are free to decide what to do with it. As the impulse of imitation is strong, there is no expectation that the parents compel their child to join in, rather that they do so themselves. The parents do not only sit and chat with each other, but also play with their children. When they are involved in a craft, however, the children either join them out of imitation, or it allows the children the space and freedom to begin their own more social exploration.

The toys used are simple, as in the kindergarten. Carved wooden animals and toys, hand-sewn dolls, and natural objects found on walks, e.g. conkers, pine cones and sea shells. Lengths of dyed muslin are wrapped around screens to form cosy home corners and little dens.

The making of simple crafts help the parents to recognise skills and to bring some of these into their home, such as baking bread, painting and drawing. Nature tables in the home are encouraged, and seasonal crafts, such as the butterflies, mobiles, lanterns and decorations which the children make, enhance these. Parent and child sit together, work together and learn together, handling the simplest of natural materials,

Figure 11.2 Parent and child group

such as brightly coloured sheep's wool, cones and seeds, beeswax, muslin and silk.

In each session there is time for play and craft activity, which run alongside each other for around an hour. A tidy-up song forms the prelude to ring time. Here the children and parents may listen to the story of a little child and the journey made from home to countryside and back home again, via the animals in the fields and the woods or rivers, mixed with the familiar nursery rhymes and seasonal songs of childhood. Touch is encouraged between parent and child; hand-gesture games, movement and sometimes puppets are enjoyed. Properly seated around the table, a snack of freshly baked food is shared, once the blessing has been sung, as a reminder of the importance of sharing with one another.

The morning finishes with time in the garden, and a meeting later in the goodbye circle, which is both an affirmation of time together, as well as a reminder of future meetings.

It is recognised that parenting is the most important task that each of us can do, and therefore support and guidance is given where necessary or required.

The transition from a parent and child group into kindergarten is an easy one, both for the child and for the parent. They are already settled into a rhythm, know how to eat together, have shared festivals and celebrations, and are familiar with songs. The parents are also already familiar with the Steiner approach to parenting, and with the expectations and ethos of the Steiner Waldorf approach to both parenting and the education.

Childminding and home childcare

There are now Steiner-trained childminders active throughout the UK. They usually work from home, and provide a similar routine to the kindergarten, although this can be for the whole day. These are in a genuine homely environment and also include mixed-age groups, which might be from baby to eight years depending on the situation. Some of these are held outdoors or in yurts. Many childminders support a local school community.

The integration of the Pikler approach in work with the very young child

Dr Emmi Pikler (1902–1984) qualified as a paediatrician in Hungary. She developed an approach to the child, which was based on building an authentic, respectful relationship. She founded Loczy, an orphanage in Budapest, which is now known as the Pikler Institute, and her daughter Anna Tardos has continued this approach, turning Loczy into a day-care centre and a training centre for pedagogues and parents. After many years training with Dr Pikler, Magda Gerber established her own movement in America, known as Resources for Infant Educarers (RIE).

Figure 11.3 Gentle beginnings

107

There are many similarities with the Steiner Waldorf approach, particularly the respectful care of the child, and acknowledging time and space for the child to have the possibility for naturally paced motor development and free self-directed movement. Steiner parent and baby groups work with this, particularly in developing observational skills and strengthening attachment between parent and child.

Dorothy Marlen pioneered an approach to parent support in the first eighteen months of a child's life. She called it 'Gentle Beginnings' and was inspired by the Pikler approach. Dorothy is also one of the founders of the UK Pikler Association, and brought the Pikler training to the UK.

12 | Other subjects

Eurythmy

Eurythmy as a subject is part of the Steiner Waldorf school curriculum from kindergarten through to the 12th class. It is an art of movement that is used both for education and also for artistic performance.

Eurythmy requires that we become inwardly mobile. When we hear sounds, we are taken along into continuous change, from high to low, from soft to loud. We are also carried along on the course of a melody, in changes of melody and melodic moods, and in the subtleties of spoken language. In Eurythmy these changes and their related inner movements are made manifest by movements of the body. This is done both individually and in groups. In doing Eurythmy the body becomes an instrument, visualising what is otherwise only audible; namely, music and speech.

First do then think

The awareness of one's own body is the beginning of self-knowledge. This awareness is acquired by being active, by moving. Through movement and activity children get to know their environment and become acquainted with the things around them, as well as their own functioning body. In all the movements through which they interact with their surroundings, their own body is the firm reference point.

While thinking we also move, not physically but mentally. The inner movements we make while thinking can be compared to the outer

Figure 12.1 Eurythmy

movements we make while exploring something physically. In Steiner education these two processes are continually interconnected, not just because children like to move, but because learning processes backed up by movement obtain meaning. Thinking and doing are connected.

In performing Eurythmy gestures we visualise the movement of the creative forces that precede language and music. We enter into the moment at which language and music are still incipient. When we sing we are able to sense this movement while going from one tone to the next. Singing the first tone, we already move inwardly towards the following one. We then perceive how the subsequent tone must first be found; the movement towards must be discovered before that tone can sound in tune. These are the same creative movements as the ones we visualise with our entire body in Eurythmy. During Eurythmy lessons the children enter into the creative movements of language and music through their own movements.

Rudolf Steiner pointed out how the creative movements we use in language and music are related to the creative life forces active in nature, as well as to those that work in our physical organism. When we do Eurythmy with children we address these life forces.

Eurythmy therapy

Eurythmy therapy may be used to help a child with learning difficulties or developmental problems. Specific exercises are given to individual children to help them with their physical and inner development. This type of Eurythmy is prescribed by the Steiner school doctor and given by a specially trained Curative Eurythmist.

Languages

Languages are introduced early in the kindergarten. Children are at their most receptive in the early years, and if a new language is brought into their daily life in some way, we help to develop their ear to take in new sounds, in the same way that it develops musically. The introduction of languages is done during ring time through song, rhyme, finger games or circle games, or in the morning, before an activity. The teacher or assistant needs to have a good understanding of the language, and needs to be able to pronounce it accurately, for if the children are learning out of imitation, what they are imitating needs to be correct! This works in the same way as the introduction of English as a second language to those children new to English. If the staff are not familiar with any other languages, a guest, parent or specialist teacher is sometimes invited to participate in the ring time, or in a morning activity.

Television and the media

TV is embedded in our culture and taken for granted to such a degree that it is often difficult for us to question its value. Similarly, with the increasing prominence of cinema, the personal computer, tablets and video games, and their adoption into everyday life, rarely is a dissenting voice heard. However, it is widely held among those involved in Steiner education, as well as by researchers worldwide, that watching TV and videos, playing computer games and overuse of electronic technology are detrimental to the healthy development of the child. Our reasons for this are that all children have an innate imaginative capacity and their natural state is to be active in this. This is one of the great gifts of childhood and crucial for children's healthy journey into adulthood, when children acquire other faculties. As they do so, it is a capacity which is usually lost or transformed, never to be relived in the same way. TV, videos, computer games, etc. make children unhealthily 'still' and stifle their own imaginations. By presenting the child with 'finished' images, the child is required to do no inner work (or active play) at all, and their imagination is 'disabled' while watching. Afterwards, this can result in listlessness, lack of initiative and boredom; children may need to be constantly entertained. Alternatively, it may result in children being overstimulated to such an extent that they can no longer listen properly to real people: they switch on or off as they please. It is felt that this kind of stimulation is in fact *deprivation* for the child's own abundant creative abilities.

Through Steiner Waldorf education, we encourage children's natural capacity to be highly sensitive to their environment and the people around them. They are, therefore, deeply susceptible to being mesmerised: they cannot filter their absorption of the things they see and hear. We are careful in both the kindergarten and school to present material in a way appropriate to their age and sensibilities. By contrast, the quality of children's material on TV, videos and computers is often very poor, forcing images and noises of all kinds upon the child which are, in our view, inappropriate. The children may become desensitised as their threshold for violence, noise, aesthetics, moral and social behaviour decreases. Young children do not have the ability to discriminate and regulate their own watching. They are not yet able to know what is good for them and what is not, and depend on the adults around them to decide the boundaries which will protect them (in all areas of life, not just this one) until they can freely take care of themselves.

Furthermore, the images that flash past on the screen are not connected to real life: they are an artificial representation of life and, as such, abstract. One cannot *relate* to TV. Children live vividly in the present and to be healthy they need to feel deeply connected to the world around them. They do not have the intellectual sophistication to cope healthily with this abstract phenomenon.

Children are discouraged from watching television or playing on computers, and if at all, only to watch at the weekend.

Conclusion

In Steiner education, we try to make our kindergartens a haven for the young child. Our unwritten motto over the door is 'Here we have time' . . . time for the children to experience themselves and others, and grow in peace and harmony; where the child feels safe and not under pressure to perform or compete; where we weave a tapestry of learning experiences for the child. That is the ideal in a Steiner Waldorf kindergarten.

Figure 12.2 Here we have time

Appendix 1

Exemptions and modifications to EYFS 2014

Below is the chart of exemptions applied for by all Steiner early childhood settings, including childminders.

EXEMPTIONS AND MODIFICATIONS REQUESTED FROM THE LEARNING AND DEVELOPMENT REQUIREMENT & ELG/EYFSP

In the exemptions application form, we have asked to explain why exemption is needed and how the exemption will affect children's experience: *In brief and to add to the information below:* Parents carefully and deliberately choose Steiner education in order to give their children a broad, rich and imaginative early childhood experience in mixed age groups. The education and care is holistic, enabling and provides for their diverse skills and abilities, concentration and enthusiasm. They do not acquire skills through any formal or teacher directed learning, but at their own pace through the example of well trained and competent adults in an enabling environment in which they develop life skills and which offers effective foundations for later formal learning. The children transfer to Steiner (or Primary) schools socially competent and good communicators, with excellent physical abilities and skills. They are generally enthusiastic and able to give purpose and direction to their lifelong learning.

The learning and development requirement (educational programme, early learning goal, profile assessment) affected	Exemption/modification requested	Rationale
Communication and Language **Understanding:** Children follow instructions involving several ideas or actions. They answer 'how' and 'why' questions about their experiences and in response to stories or events.	b) **Understanding:** Children follow instructions involving several ideas or actions. **They demonstrate understanding in response to stories or events or when recounting their experiences.**	The Steiner EY curriculum seeks to nurture and protect the child's imaginative world and direct teaching, questioning and reminding is seen as running counter to this. Although the teachers may answer children's questions, these initially stem from the child's own experiences and self-initiated learning. Teachers do not ask how and why questions to stimulate consciousness, or extend learning.

(continued)

(continued)

The learning and development requirement (educational programme, early learning goal, profile assessment) affected	Exemption/modification requested	Rationale
Physical development. Moving and handling: Children show good control and co-ordination in large and small movements. They move confidently in a range of ways, safely negotiating space. They handle equipment and tools effectively, including pencils for writing.	Children show good control and co-ordination in large and small movements. They move confidently in a range of ways, safely negotiating space. They handle equipment and tools effectively, including **crayons for mark making.**	As children are not taught to read and write before rising 7 in the Steiner Setting, they are not provided with a full range of writing materials or any formal instruction. Children have the opportunity for mark making as in most cases crayons and paper is available. A range of arts and crafts contribute to the development of fine motor skills necessary for writing in the future.
Mathematics Numbers: Children count reliably with numbers from 1 to 20, place them in order and say which number is one more or one less than a given number. Using quantities and objects, they add and subtract two single-digit numbers and count on or back to find the answer. They solve problems, including doubling, halving and sharing.	Children **orally** count reliably with numbers from 1 to 20, place them in order and say which number is one more or one less than a given number. Using quantities and objects they add and subtract two single-digit numbers and count on or back to find the answer. **In everyday activities and play they solve problems,** including doubling, halving and sharing.	Steiner settings do not teach number recognition (from written numerals) or written number formation before rising 7. Steiner children might not have the opportunity to see or recognize written numbers: there are generally no clocks, the scales used are generally balance scales, and measuring is done without using measuring jugs with numbers. It is an established principle in the Steiner EY curriculum that a sound foundation for grasping mathematical concepts comes from allowing the young child to first experience opportunities to count, calculate and problem solve in naturally occurring everyday situations.

Understanding the world

Technology: Children recognise that a range of technology is used in places such as homes and schools. They select and use technology for particular purposes.

Children recognise that a range of **simple or mechanical everyday technology** is used in places such as homes and schools. They select and use technology for particular purposes.

The Steiner EY curriculum integrates mathematical concepts and uses mathematical language and concepts through regular everyday activities and routines of the kindergarten that involve the child in, for example; pairing up the shoes when tidying up; weighing and measuring ingredients when preparing food, counting plates when setting the table for snack time.

The Steiner belief is that electronic technology, such as TV, computers, tape recorders or electronic toys runs counter to their aim to develop the imagination and nurture the child's cognitive capacities by physically learning through doing. Children instead use technology that provides direct experiences enabling them to gain knowledge of how things work.

Computers are only introduced later in the Steiner curriculum on the grounds that passive activity is not healthy; it takes away time to play; there are problems associated with young children dwelling in virtual reality that can lead to confusion/distortion of values and that it can lead to the over-reliance on the computer as a teaching/learning tool.

(continued)

(continued)

The learning and development requirement (educational programme, early learning goal, profile assessment) affected	Exemption/modification requested	Rationale
Expressive arts and design **Being imaginative:** Children use what they have learnt about media and materials in original ways, thinking about uses and purposes. They represent their own ideas, thoughts and feelings through design and technology, art, music, dance, role play and stories.	Children use what they have learnt about media and materials in original ways, thinking about uses and purposes. They represent their own ideas, thoughts and feelings through design and **non-electronic** technology, art, music, dance, role play and stories.	Steiner site that research has shown that human speech and live music have many advantages over recorded speech or music in that all the senses of the child are addressed at the same time and that live music supports the development of the brain. They also believe that recorded sound is not necessary in a setting where the human voice is heard. The Steiner belief is that electronic technology, such as TV, computers, tape recorders or electronic toys counter the effect of their aim to develop the imagination and nurture the child's human relationship to others.

Literacy
The Programme is:

Literacy development involves encouraging children to link sounds and letters and to begin to read and write. Children must be given access to a wide range of reading materials (books, poems, and other written materials) to ignite their interest.

The two goals are:

i) Reading: Children read and understand simple sentences. They use phonic knowledge to decode regular words and read them aloud accurately. They also read some common irregular words. They demonstrate understanding when talking with others about what they have read.

Complete exemption from the whole literacy educational programme.

It is an established principle in Steiner EY curriculum that young children are not taught to read and write before rising 7. Children are told stories rather than read to because the spoken, rather than the printed word, allows the teachers to tell the story in their own words to suit the group of children in their care, and for the children to develop their own imaginary pictures to accompany the story, as well as to develop concentration and a broad vocabulary from the stories told. Steiner say that well-chosen words and good syntax support clear thinking and lay secure foundations for developing language and literacy.

The Steiner curriculum introduces formal reading and writing at a later age preferring in the early years to put in place the foundations for reading and writing through developing listening skills and exploring sounds through speech development, and developing fine motor skills through play and everyday activities.

(continued)

(continued)

The learning and development requirement (educational programme, early learning goal, profile assessment) affected	Exemption/modification requested	Rationale
j) **Writing:** Children use their phonic knowledge to write words in ways which match their spoken sounds. They also write some irregular common words. They write simple sentences which can be read by themselves and others. Some words are spelt correctly and others are phonetically plausible.		Children have the opportunity for mark making, but the written word is not formally introduced, although the child's self-initiated writing is supported by the teacher when asked by the child. In most cases children do not have access to pencils, rather the preferred **Steiner** block or stick crayons are used. The books available are mostly picture books and children are encouraged to 'read the pictures' using their imagination stimulated by the pictures. The children know that print carries meaning from seeing adults using writing in the daily routine of the kindergarten. Children's language development is encouraged by the teacher modelling good language during every day activities, a broad vocabulary through storytelling, and using a range of poems, songs and stories in a daily movement and music session.

| ASSESSMENT AT THE END OF THE EYFS: THE EARLY YEARS FOUNDATION STAGE PROFILE (2.6–2.11) | **Complete exemption from the whole section on assessment at the end of the EYFS –Early Years Foundation Stage profile**
2.6: completion of the profile including 2.7; 2.8; 2.9; 2.10
2.11: submitting profile to LA | Steiner conduct their own continuous observational assessment of the social, physical, spiritual and emotional development of the whole child in accordance with the Steiner ethos' developmental stages of the child. Observational assessments, which are usually recorded in a Steiner child profile, is an integral part of their practice and is an essential tool for practitioners in order to gain an overview of the child. The profile is particularly relevant when the child is about to move up to Class 1 (age 6+) in the Steiner school, where a summative evaluation of the child is passed on to the Class 1 teacher and shared with parents. The child's developmental progress is discussed regularly with parents in the form of individual meetings and written reports. |

(continued)

(continued)

The learning and development requirement (educational programme, early learning goal, profile assessment) affected	Exemption/modification requested	Rationale
		To complete and submit the EYFS profile against goals, some of which conflict with the Steiner curriculum, (and from which they are exempt), is incompatible with their method of assessment. The children from schools that have requested exemption from the profile generally remain in Steiner schools and continue to Class 1 at rising 7 therefore the profile is not needed to inform Reception or Year 1 teachers in mainstream schools. If they do transfer to other schools, a thorough report is given to the next teacher via the parents.

Parents also object to their child being assessed and the data collection on a set of goals (the ELG profile scores) which are not fundamental to Steiner Waldorf ethos and practice. |

Appendix 2

Relevant organisations

Steiner Waldorf Schools Fellowship (SWSF)

The Steiner Waldorf Schools Fellowship (SWSF) represents Steiner or Waldorf education in the UK and Ireland. It is a registered charity and carries responsibility for: advice; curriculum research; quality care and accreditation; support for legal and administrative matters, conferences, teacher training, contact with national media; international information, publishing and translating resource material, books and articles and a termly *Newsletter*. SWSF holds the trademark on the use of the names (Rudolf) Steiner or Waldorf in the context of education.

Website: www.steinerwaldorf.org

Accreditation

All full member and sponsored schools are registered charities regulated by the Charity Commission or relevant body. All schools and independent kindergartens are also registered with the requisite agencies of government and are inspected accordingly (by Ofsted, Estyn, and HMIe etc.). Different arrangements, however, apply to schools in the Republic of Ireland. In addition to national regulations. member institutions receive advisory support and accreditation through the Fellowship. Full member schools seek to apply a range and depth of quality indicators included in the Fellowship's Code of Practice, and through shared good practice. 'Sponsored' schools and provisionally registered kindergartens are projects developing towards full membership and receive regular accreditation visits from experienced colleagues. There is a category for Steiner-inspired childminders, and a list of parent and child groups.

There is a small number of initiatives or interest groups working with elements of Steiner education, or using them for home education. These are non-accredited. Affiliate activities are similarly not accredited, such as schools or organisations with compatible aims and objectives in mutually supportive communication with SWSF; for example, the European Council for Steiner Waldorf Education (http: www.ecswe. org). Each school is expected to implement the Fellowship Code of Practice for administration and management.

The world list of Steiner Waldorf schools can be found on: http:// www.waldorfschule.info/upload/pdf/schulliste.pdf.

Special educational needs and Camphill communities

There are also a number of related, unaccredited foundations affiliated to the Fellowship. SWSF schools should be distinguished from the homes, schools and communities for children and young people in the Steiner Education Special Schools sector, and apply an adapted Waldorf curriculum. For further information, contact:

- The Association of Camphill Communities
  - **Tel:** 01653 694197
  - **Email:** info@camphill.org.uk

All SWSF schools are day schools but home boarding can be arranged at some schools.

Teacher training in Steiner Waldorf early childhood

A range of teacher education pathways is currently available in the Steiner Waldorf movement in Britain and Ireland. Provision includes publicly and privately funded courses which lead to Steiner Waldorf early childhood qualifications, recognised in the framework of historical and nationally recognised qualifications. The SWSF supports courses and programmes seeking forms of public accreditation. All courses are administratively independent of SWSF.

The three early years training courses (all of which are awarded by the Council for Awards in Care, Health and Education (CACHE) and carry the Early Years Educator (EYE) qualification) are part-time and partly work-based. You can find direct links to them from the Steiner Waldorf Schools Fellowship website (http://www.steinerwaldorf.org/steiner-teachers/teacher-education).

There are also part-time courses for parent and child group leaders, playgroup leaders, parents, childminders and anyone interested in the first three years of childhood.

Affiliated organisations

International Association for Steiner Waldorf Early Childhood Education (IASWECE)

www.iaswece.org

IASWECE represents the worldwide Steiner Waldorf early childhood movement. The goals are to:

- Foster cooperation among colleagues throughout the world, through meetings, conferences, working groups, etc.;
- Deepen and renew the work with the young child out of the sources of Waldorf education, and support for its quality;
- Foster training and continuing development opportunities for caregivers, kindergarten teachers and educators;
- Undertake and support collaborative research on contemporary questions regarding the care and education of the young child;
- Collaborate with parents, other educators and wider society about the needs of the young child;
- Protect the freedom and name of Steiner and Waldorf early childhood education;

- Provide resources, information and publications on Waldorf early childhood education;
- Offer support – human, educational and financial – for projects seeking to foster Waldorf early childhood education throughout the world.

The Alliance for Childhood (United Kingdom)

www.allianceforchildhood.org.uk

The Alliance for Childhood is a worldwide network of individuals and organisations committed to fostering and respecting each child's inherent right to a healthy childhood, and serves as a network that facilitates reflection and action by people with concerns about the care and education of children.

It is not a conventional organisation, but involves an engagement in working together for the betterment of the experience of childhood. It exists in the shared work and spirit of cooperation, whereby all partners can find mutual support.

Aims and objectives of the current partners of the Alliance for Childhood are to:

- support family life;
- promote a developmentally appropriate Early Years curriculum;
- work for the better physical and emotional health of children;
- fight poverty and neglect in all forms;
- question the role of electronic media in child development;
- highlight the dangers of commercialism aimed at children;
- improve childcare facilities.

The Pikler Association

www.pikler.co.uk

Dorothy Marlen

www.dorothymarlen.net

Irish Steiner Kindergarten Association (ISKA)

Supporting Steiner Waldorf early childhood education and care in Ireland.

http://www.iskaireland.org/

Bibliography and resources

Bibliography

Alliance for Childhood (2000) *The Future of Childhood*. Stroud, UK: Hawthorn Press.

Baldwin, D. R. (2004) *You Are Your Child's First Teacher*. Stroud, UK: Hawthorn Press.

Ball, C. (1994) *The Start Right Document*. London: Royal Society of Arts.

Bettelheim, B. (1991) *The Uses of Enchantment: The Meaning and Importance of Fairy Tales*. London: Penguin Psychology.

Brown, B. (1998) *Unlearning Discrimination in the Early Years*. London: Trentham Books.

Bruce, T. (2005) *Early Childhood Education*. Oxon, UK: Hodder and Stoughton.

Bryer, E. (2011) *Movement for the Young Child*. Spring Valley, NY: Waldorf Early Childhood Association of North America (WECAN).

Carey, D. and Large, J. (2001) *Festivals, Family and Food*. Stroud, UK: Hawthorn Press.

Clouder, C., Jenkinson, S. and Large, M. (2001) *The Future of Childhood*. Sussex, UK: SWSF Publications.

Clouder, C. and Nicol, J. (2008) *Creative Play for Your Toddler*. London: Gaia.

Clouder, C. and Nicol, J. (2007) *Creative Play for Your Baby*. London: Gaia.

Druitt, A., Fynes-Clinton, C. and Rowling, M. (1995) *All Year Round*. Stroud, UK: Hawthorn Press.

Early Years Foundation Stage (2014). Available online at: www.gov.uk/government/publications (Reference: DFE-00337-2014).

Elkind, D. (2014) *Giants in the Nursery*. St. Paul, MN: Redleaf Press.

Glockler, M. and Goebel, A. (2012) *Guide to Child Health*. Edinburgh: Floris Books.

Jaffke, F. (2002) *Work and Play in early Childhood*. Edinburgh, UK: Floris Books.

Jaffke, F. (2002) *Toymaking with Children*. Edinburgh, UK: Floris Books.

Jenkinson, S. (2006) On the Seashore of Worlds, *KINDLING*, Issue 9, p.6.

Jenkinson, S. (2001) *The Genius of Play: Celebrating the Spirit of Childhood.* Stroud, UK: Hawthorn Press.

Klugman, E. and Smilansky, S. (1990) *Children's Play and Learning.* New York, NY: Teacher's College Press.

Lissau, R. (1987) *Rudolf Steiner: His Life, Work, Inner Path and Social Initiatives.* Stroud, UK: Hawthorn Press.

Male, D. (2005) *The Parent and Child Group Handbook: A Steiner/Waldorf Approach.* Stroud, UK: Hawthorn Press.

Mellon, N. (2001) *Storytelling with Children.* Stroud, UK: Hawthorn Press.

Molt, E. and Murphy, C. (1991) *Emil Molt and the Beginnings of the First Waldorf School.* Edinburgh, UK: Floris Books.

Muller, B. (1987) *Painting with Children.* Edinburgh, UK: Floris Books.

Nicol, J. and Taplin, J. (2012) *Understanding the Steiner Waldorf Approach.* Oxon, UK: Routledge.

Nutbrown, C. (2008) *Early Childhood Education: History, Philosophy and Experience.* London: Sage.

Nutbrown, C. (2006) *Key Concepts in Early Childhood Education and Care.* London: Sage.

Oldfield, L. (2013) *Free to Learn.* Stroud: Hawthorn Press.

Parker-Rees, R. (ed.) (2011) *Meeting the Child in Steiner Kindergartens: An Exploration of Beliefs, Values and Practices.* London: Routledge.

Salter, J. (1992) *The Incarnating Child.* Stroud, UK: Hawthorn Press.

Schweizer, S. (2009) *Under the Sky.* London: Rudolf Steiner Press.

Schweizer, S. (2007) *Well, I wonder.* London: Rudolf Steiner Press.

Steiner, R. (2008) *Educating Children Today.* London: Rudolf Steiner Press.

Steiner, R. (2001) *The Foundations of Human Experience: Study of Man.* London: Rudolf Steiner Press.

Steiner, R. (1998) *The Child's Changing Consciousness.* London: Rudolf Steiner Press.

Steiner, R. (1996) *The Education of the Child.* Hudson, NY: Anthroposophic Press.

Steiner, R. (1972) *A Modern Art of Education.* London: Rudolf Steiner Press.

Steiner, R. (1968) *The Roots of Education.* London: Rudolf Steiner Press.

Strauss, M. (2007) *Understanding Children's Drawings.* London: Rudolf Steiner Press.

Von Heydenbrand, C. (2001) *Childhood.* London: Rudolf Steiner Press.

Von Kugelgen, H. (1993) Fairytale Language and the Image of Man, in *An Overview of the Waldorf Kindergarten,* Vol.1. Spring Valley, NY: WECAN.

Whitebread, D., Basilio, M., Kuvalja, M. and Verma, M. (2012) The Importance of Play. Available at: http://www.importanceofplay.eu/IMG/pdf/dr_david_whitebread_-_the_importance_of_play.pdf.

Wynstones Collection (see 'Collections and anthologies').

Collections and anthologies

Acorn Hill Anthology of Songs and Stories: Let us form a Ring (Vol. 1) and *Dancing as we sing* (Vol. 2). Spring Valley, NY: WECAN.
Gesture Games, by Wilma Ellersierk. New York, NY: WECAN (distributed by Floris Books).
Nature and Seasonal Crafts Series: *Spring, Summer, Autumn, Winter, The Nature Corner, Christmas, Easter*, and other titles. Edinburgh: Floris Books.
Wynstones Collection: *Spring, Summer, Autumn, Winter, Spindrift* and *Gateways* (songs, stories, poems, verses, fairy tales, birthdays etc.). Stroud, UK: Wynstones Press.

Journals and compilations

A Deeper Understanding of the Waldorf Kindergarten. Spring Valley, NY: WECAN.
An Overview of the Waldorf Kindergarten, Vols. 1 and 2. Spring Valley, NY: WECAN.
Juno: A natural approach to family life. www.junomagazine.com.
KINDLING: the Journal for Steiner Waldorf Early Childhood Education and Care, UK. http://www.steinerwaldorf.org/steiner-education/early-years/kindling-journal/.
The Young Child in the World Today. Spring Valley, NY: WECAN.

Useful websites

Steiner Waldorf Schools Fellowship: www.steinerwaldorf.org
Waldorf Answers on the philopsophy and practice of Waldorf education: www.waldorfanswers.org
The online Waldorf library: www.waldorflibrary.org

Resources for craft materials, toys, healthcare and Waldorf equipment

Mercurius: www.mercurius-international.com
Myriad Natural Toys: www.myriadonline.co.uk
Weleda (UK) Ltd: www.weleda.co.uk